Look
and See

Published by The Buddhist Society
Patron: His Holiness the Dalai Lama
Registered Charity No. 1113705

Published by The Buddhist Society, 2017
© The Buddhist Society, 2017
Text © The Zen Trust

This publication has been generously supported
by The Hokun Trust and The Zen Centre, London

ISBN: 978-0-901032-46-1 (The Buddhist Society)

A catalogue record for this book is available from the British Library

Translation and Commentary by Venerable Myokyo-ni
Edited by Sarah Auld
Designed by Avni Patel

Printed in Padstow, Cornwall by TJ International

The Buddhist Society
58 Eccleston Square
London
SW1V 1PH
T: 020 7834 5858
E: info@thebuddhistsociety.org
thebuddhistsociety.org

Look
and See

Buddhist Teaching Stories
with Commentaries by the
Venerable Myokyo-ni

Fragrance
of the Dharma
Hōkun Trust

CONTENTS

6

Foreword, Desmond Biddulph

9

Introduction, Venerable Myokyo-ni

20

CHAPTER I From the Southern Scriptures

1 Kisa Gotami
2 The Parable of the Poisoned Arrow
3 The Pleasant Downy Creeper
4 The Blind Men and the Elephant
5 The Monkey and the Pitch Trap
6 The Ass in the Lion's Skin – 'Nay this is not a Lion's Roar'
7 Excess of Zeal
8 On Getting Angry
9 The Anger-eating Demon
10 The Bare Bones
11 Death's Three Messengers
12 The Forest Dweller
13 A Life free from Passion is not Bland
14 Seeing but not being Deceived by Form
15 The Parable of the Raft

81

CHAPTER II From the Northern Training Scriptures

16 The Two Ships
17 The Lost Son
18 The Tree-Pruning Master
19 The Spider
20 The Great Wave
21 The Taming of the Harp
22 An Old Man of Eighty
23 The Thousand-foot Cliff

111

CHAPTER III The One Way

24 Step Carefully
25 The Parable of the Smouldering Anthill

FOREWORD

The author was a lifelong teacher at the Buddhist Society, head of two Rinzai Zen training monasteries in England, and probably the leading teacher in that tradition for decades until her death in 2007. A pioneer of Zen in the West following in the footsteps of DT Suzuki and Christmas Humphreys, who after twelve years in Daitokuji training monastery, returned to teach the true Dharma. The author's excellent introduction firmly locates these stories within the cultural framework of Far Eastern Buddhism, influenced as it is by the Dao, and Confucianism, yet never departing from the fundamental insight of Shakyamuni Buddha's enlightenment.

All that is 'grave and constant in human experience' is met in this single life, but whether we experience it, or turn a blind eye to it, is a matter of primary concern to all those who recognise the mystery and majesty of life, and value the remarkable gift that it is.

The whole of the Buddha's teaching could be summarised in the phrase 'Look and See', and so this book points, not only to the function of 'looking' and 'seeing,' so central to the Buddha's message, but to a practice enshrined as a pillar of Buddhist teachings; meditation. What is met in meditation practice arises from a life fully lived, and so to meet these grave and constant human emotions, and for them to be fully seen into, requires the cultivation of particular qualities. A practical approach to both the mastery of ourselves, spoken of as morality, and the cultivation of meditation, leads to both a deeper commitment to life itself, as well as an enhanced capacity for understanding, and feeling for all life, with which we share this tiny place in the vast deserts of this seemingly empty cosmos.

We can look to the ends of the universe, and we do, and find much of fascination there, even solace, when faced with the vastness of it, but we do not find the answer to the existential problems of life, nor the strength and flexibility we need when in a crisis. To look 'to the place where our own feet stand' as urged to by the Zen masters of old, is so much more difficult then looking outward, yet it is where we are right now that we urgently need to look; but how? This book makes the 'looking' so much easier and can open the path to a lifelong spiritual journey. A journey through life that we all make anyway, whether we like it or not, that time between birth and death, with the light and dark that comes our way.

The book says, do not be afraid; in the darkness, there is light, and light is replaced by darkness in due course, itself to be replaced again, but underneath this lies an enduring luminosity, life after life. The strength and fearlessness we need to live fully, with open eyes, open hands and open hearts, is not easily achieved, yet, when achieved through practice, unless tempered by a spiritual path, can lead to our downfall, and the suffering of others. Those readers interested in life as a spiritual journey and specifically as seen through the lens of the Buddha Dharma will find much of what they seek, within the covers of this modest book.

The Buddha proclaimed, on seeing the morning star, after so many years of struggle, 'How wonderful, how miraculous – all beings are fully endowed with the wisdom and power of the Tathāgata – but sadly human beings, on account of their sticky attachments, are not aware of it'.

This little book, filled with so many stories, the essence of which we all recognise, helps the spiritual pilgrim on his way.

Desmond Biddulph
President, The Buddhist Society
London, 2016

INTRODUCTION

The seeds of this little book were sown – or sowed them-selves – some thirty years ago on a cargo ship. I was a 'pupil without a master', that is after the death of Sesso Roshi I had come back to London for a short visit and was now returning to resume training under his successor. The first evening out, my neighbour at table offered to share his bottle of wine and by way of getting acquainted told me over dinner that he regularly did such round trips. He had been a police officer in India, was long retired, his children well-to-do and his wife had died a few years ago. In short, he was lonely and such voyages provided interest and new companions. The few other passengers seemed to be similarly moti-vated – truly 'all in the same boat'. I wanted to reply, to say something sympathetic and encouraging to my neighbour, only to realize that after so many years of involvement in Buddhism and six years of training in a traditional Japanese Zen monastery, my vocabulary and mode of expression was almost exclusively Buddhist and as such would be a dis-cordant note in the small group of lonely people willy-nilly together for weeks. So I resorted to my usual way of resolving a dilemma – I shut myself up to hatch it out. True enough, on the third day it 'broke', that is it broke in on me with overwhelming force what a fool I was. I had been spouting Buddhist vocabulary for years without realizing that it was but a shorthand-code for our common problems, dilem-mas, and sorrows for all that is grave and constant in human experience. With a fellow Buddhist this code sufficed, but it could just as well be translated into ordinary language and be of benefit to all.

With that I sauntered forth into the ship's life, chastened but cheerfully, and now having the 'key', could freely talk about common human problems such as age, loneliness, etc., and how to conducively view and confront these with a positive attitude that might help towards peace of mind and warmth of heart, even a new interest in life. For just that is the message of the Buddha's teachings.

Stories and parables are an integral part of traditional teaching texts. They are of such simplicity that one is inclined to smile at them as rather childish and as of no relevance to our lives today. Yet on closer acquaintance they reveal a profound insight into human nature, expound perennial verities and serve as pointers or guides. They console, succour, direct towards a more conducive attitude and a fuller, more meaningful partaking in life. This in its turn engenders vigour and strength that enlivens the individual and opens the heart in compassionate understanding towards its fellow beings. Such partaking in life as a true human being also means being aware of and in tune with all that is, 'at one' again with the Essence of Being which 'informs' all forms as their inherent laws. This is the insight to which the man Gautama 'awoke' and thus became the Buddha, the 'All-Wise and All Compassionate One' – for these two aspects are intrinsically intertwined.

It is, of course, not possible to define what this insight is or what it consists of. The teachings only set out the way that is to be walked towards this insight, and the parables and analogies are picture-maps of the stages and pitfalls on this way. This they do in a direct, concrete and refreshingly earthy manner, yet embedded in them is also a deeper, more universal resonance to which the human heart seems to incline, and on merging with which it fulfils itself. All I-centred thought mistakes this inclination for 'I want', and this misunderstanding is an ever-fruitful source of our common dilemmas, of our sorrows, quarrels, fights, grievances, agitations, frustrations, anxieties, fears – the list is endless.

A child has just cut its finger, blood is dripping, it howls in shock and pain. Surely the first response to that is a hug, 'there, there', and putting on a plaster; the child is reassured, comforted and soon forgets its shock. Now is the time to remind it, 'How often have you been told not to play with that knife – now you see what happens'. We all are such children; although in a way we always know, yet under the sway of strong impulses we tend to act heedless of what we know. And so we have simple, seemingly obvious stories in all traditions. These embody millennia of human experience and act in a twofold way, giving comfort and succour at the moment while at the same time pointing at something beyond, something dimly sensed in our better moments but usually swamped by excess of emotional reaction – or stubborn insistence – like the child with the knife.

The stories presented in this volume are collected from various Buddhist sources but have in common the Buddhist way of facing the 'Trials of Life'. These latter are all too familiar, but when suddenly seen from a quite different, i.e. the Buddhist, angle they may jolt us and open up what hitherto had eluded us. This results in a clearer perception, a more appropriate attitude, and consequently prompts action that, more adapted to the situation as it is, is less stressful, more 'at ease'.

In Buddhism, the common human experience is expressed as 'Parting from what we like, having what we do not like' in an ever-changing round, turning from one to the other. In this, wealth, health, fame, beloved, life, etc. – and their opposites – cover all possible contingencies and individual permutations. Our life, and indeed the world we live in, we ourselves included, are diurnal, consist of light and dark, summer and winter and all the other pairs of opposites. In that sense the stage of our planet earth is 'given' or 'set', with its sun and moon, its seasonal cycles, etc. On this stage we all course, play our role and then pass on. As to that, we have no option; but how individually and/or collectively we perceive and react to what confronts us makes our weal and woe. The old joke of whether we perceive the same glass as half full or half empty illustrates this well.

Since nobody finds it difficult to enjoy the bright in life, we may for the time being forget it and consider the dark side of life, its pain, sorrow, loss and fear. There the message comes across that in each of these painful experiences is a chance of transformation. The latter can be aimed at and worked towards along specific paths, but it can also happen out of the blue or at times of deepest need and despair. What I see as my unbearable fate or burden, and which causes bitter resentment, 'why should it happen to me?, why me?' this acts like a poison in me; it spoils, embitters or rigidifies, in short, separates 'me alone' out of the web of our commonality, which further increases my lonely bitterness – and so on, a vicious circle. Yet the same event, however painful, even horrendous, may become the means of a total transformation far beyond my possible understanding, indeed, beyond any understanding that we ordinary people can muster. In all religions, the stories of saints and sages point out such transformations, and the trials and tribulations that had led to them. Which is not to say that trials and tribulations as such lead to transformation; on the contrary, without relevant preparation and without faith they are prone to go the 'other way' towards resentment and vengeance. What then makes transformation possible?

If instead of the selfish 'why just me?' there is the realization that others, too, know grief, pain and sorrow, then, on suffering being seen as our common human lot rather than mine only, in the human heart there wells up real warmth and compassion at this rather pitiful state. Though also comprising greatness and light, this state is yet subject to so much suffering – the inevitable suffering of the nature of things, and the suffering we human beings inflict upon each other by our greed, lust, negligence, opinionatedness, or sheer ill-will. Once the awareness of suffering as our common lot arises in the human heart, the individual, bitter 'mine only' is not just forgotten but is actually transformed into the warmth of 'all of us'. At that the misguided, lonely, lost, terrified individual is re-united or 're-born' as a mature human being, standing on his own two feet and, rather than being narrowly opinionated, open-heartedly partaking in life, unselfishly available to his surroundings.

What in Buddhism is variously called enlightenment, awakening, liberation, deliverance, etc., is basically the deliverance from the limited, shallow, mean, distorted perception of 'I only', 'as it suits me' which constitutes a kind of unconscious God-Almighty complex from which most of us suffer nowadays, and liberates us equally from the unconscious assumption of an 'easy solution' 'once and for all'. Both delude us. The one into believing that there is no limit to what I or we, science or whatnot can do. The other makes us extremely gullible as to the many odd movements, trends and cults that we nowadays witness, all of which have in common an emotional high. As that, and being trendy fashion, they are seasonal, that is short-lived. True, there is an inkling of there being something more or bigger than I but without relevant training this goes into the one or the other of the two above erroneous perceptions. For a valid transformation to take place, therefore, certain conditions are required. Neither education nor a religious way can dispense with formative practices. Without them the path peters out into a wilderness.

In Buddhism this transformation is aspired to by means of the twin practices of first, obedience to rules of restraint and observances of the basic moralities, and then of the religious discipline of meditation. Five specific hindrances are said to obstruct the path of transformation. Though seemingly diverse, their common cause is seen as the one-sided attachment to an imaginary entity 'I', to 'my way' as it suits me and indeed as 'I must have it' so as to be happy. All unskilful actions and reactions arise from this misapprehension and form the base for human suffering. Even more so do these five hindrances obstruct attempts at meditation – and it is through meditation that they can be seen and their bondage broken. Since they, however, also manifest in our daily lives and wreak havoc there, we do well to keep these hindrances in mind and guard against their compulsion. They are: desire; ill will; sloth and torpor; worry and flurry; sceptical doubt.

Many parables point out the effects of these obstacles in daily life, and show ways of overcoming them. But however widespread the provenance of these stories is, they all share a common background and often contain Buddhist technical terms. The translation of some of the key terms is difficult for even if equivalents seem to exist, they may have other connotations and so mislead. One such term, usually translated as 'mind', is now also rendered as 'heart'. We believe we think with our heads, but Chinese and Pueblo Indians alike know they think with the heart! And even that is inadequate – for the quality of enlivening is also conveyed by this term, spirit or essence of life, of existence.

Another key term is desire, considered in Buddhism the cause of all our troubles. This elemental force or power, together with that of anger or hatred, and of delusion or ignorance, is seen as setting the world in motion. Thus in Buddhism, desire, sheer want, I must have, must possess and incorporate, is neither just lust with its sexual undertones, nor even aspiration which is always directed towards something more than and above 'I'. In the Buddhist context desire is perhaps best seen as an elemental drive of tremendous power – which can, and often does, grip an individual and carry him away into some blindly compulsive action which is inevitably destructive.

Again, in the Buddhist context we are often unclear about the distinction between different wants or desires. Since with these we are in the field of common human experience, there is a helpful gauge for it. If I feel I would quite like a cup of tea or coffee just now, but know that in the present situation I cannot have it, then that is just that. But when, on realizing that I cannot have that cup now, I become all hot and bothered and start scheming and planning how to procure it, even becoming convinced that I must have it to carry on at all – idiomatically, 'I'll die if I cannot have it' – just this is desire in the Buddhist sense. In Jungian Analytical Psychology, this is defined as irrational or emotional energy and clearly differentiated from the above feeling, that it would be pleasant to have a cup of tea.

Inseparably connected with this emotional energy of desire (as well as with that of delusion and anger) are the inevitable sequels that pertain to them – the planning, scheming, manipulating by fair means or foul. We just cannot let it go and, in fact, I am possessed by the energy – not 'I have it', but 'it has me'. Which explains why, in the heat of the moment I am beside myself and no longer know what I do! The events of our century alone show how catastrophic such possessions are! This inability to let go is 'sticky attachment', which is not 'mine' as I believe it to be, but rather it has – or possesses – me, it attaches me to that cup of tea and keeps me glued to it. Small wonder I cannot let it go! And it works the same whether for a cup of tea, money, job, gain, my views, my opinions – the list is endless. Whatever thus 'gets me' also 'has me'; I cannot lay it down by an act of will. I may be able to resist its promptings but cannot prevent the turbulence that it causes.

Genuine insight of the 'Way that all things really are' is the Dharma. In the Northern Tradition, the Buddha exclaims on awakening, 'How wondrous, how mysterious, all beings are fully endowed with the Buddha's wisdom and virtue. But sadly, due to their sticky attachments, human beings are not aware of this'.

Thus the Buddhist Teachings aim at a transformation brought about by training, which consists of the transition from I-biased, childish wilfulness with its concomitant tantrums, to a mature humanity capable of responsible and sustained application, dignified even in adversity. This, however, is possible only by and through the realization of true spiritual value, from which insight the fear of death recedes. In the clarity of the awareness of what is as it is, all problems come to an end.

There is much talk and speculation about such Awakening or Enlightenment as 'experience'; perhaps it would be better to conceive of it not as an experience but as a state, that is, a new attitude in and towards life in which knowing/understanding has also lost its purely intellectual quality and is realized as an immediate sympathetic perceiving (at-one-ment, insight); indivisible from that is the readiness to hold out a helping hand where needed, which is compassion.

Meanwhile, we are hung, crucified as it were, between the two poles of 'I' and 'Selfless'. Just as Tertullius assures us that the soul is naturally Christian, a Buddhist scripture says that the heart naturally inclines, tends, slides towards Nirvana. Nirvana, however otherwise defined, is itself the state of selflessness. Suffering, then, is being suspended between the two poles, torn between them. It is from this suffering that the Buddha proclaimed the Way that leads out of it. Desire, attachment, wanting – to keep or get rid of – all give rise to suffering. But, the Buddha consoles us, nothing goes on for ever; inevitably it must come to an end. Further, an end can actively be brought about by following the Way mapped out by the guide, the Buddha, who himself walked it to the end.

The stories collected here show in various ways how trials and tribulations may be used skilfully to bring suffering to an end – for the benefit of others as well as one's own. They extend over the whole field of human experience, and should the reader find the one or other story relevant to his or her present problem, and follow the indicated way out, this collection has fulfilled its purpose. Stories taken from translated texts have purposely been kept in their somewhat old-fashioned rendering, because to some this is the familiar version perhaps known by heart, and to others the unfamiliarity might startle and cause a closer scrutiny. Throughout, rather than pandering to the politically correct but linguistically awful 'he/she', 'him' has been used, standing for both 'wo+man'.

Acknowledgments: Where do thanks start? Most of the stories have been read in translation. As stories, they are nobody's possession, but without translation they would mostly have remained unknown in the West, so thanks to the translators, some dead a hundred years or more. Deepest and respectful thanks to the late successive masters of Daitoku monastery, Master Sesso and Master Sojun, under whom it was a great privilege to train. Thanks to all those who were karmically instrumental in finding the Way and assisting the walking. Thanks to those who patiently typed and retyped the manuscript, to the publisher who suggested it and kept me at it, kindly insisting, and last but not least to those who over many years have come to periodic meetings and have listened to these and like stories and found them useful in their own lives. And thanks to the friend who supplied the following present-day story. Carrying a heavy bag of groceries, she sat down to rest on a bench. A gentleman also sitting there remarked that in this wonderful summer weather he usually sat there. His home was quite a distance away, he was retired, a Muslim, and attended the mosque down the road five times a day. Then he asked her about Christian observances. On telling him that she was a Buddhist, he nodded knowledgeably, 'Ah yes, Prince Gautama who became the Buddha. And here we sit in a London suburb and his voice has reached this far. He has not lived in vain.' May the Buddha's voice reach our hearts, too, and make them respond – and may we not live in vain, but be of assistance to each other.

CHAPTER I

From the Southern Scriptures

1 *Kisa Gotami*

A young woman lost her husband soon after the birth of their first child. Though desperately poor, she was well liked in her village for being hard-working and obliging and so she and the child suffered no want. She adored her child and all went well for some years. Then disaster struck again, the child died, The poor woman was beside herself with grief – all that she had left, all that she cared for, had now been taken and she could not bear it. Loudly lamenting she ran through the village with the little dead body in her arms and refused to have it buried. The villagers tried to console her but to no avail; she was beyond reasoning. Finally the village elder suggested to her that on the next day the Lord Buddha was to preach in the neighbouring village and if she went there, he – being all-compassionate and all-wise – might make her child live again.

Very early next morning she set off for the long walk, carrying the dead child in her arms. There in front of the Buddha she knelt down and crying bitterly beseeched the Buddha to restore her child to her. The Buddha tried to make her understand that such was not in his power, but she could not listen and in anguish only reiterated her plea to make her child live again. And the Buddha, who is both all-compassionate and all-wise, finally said that he would try but needed three mustard seeds for it. Overjoyed, the woman made to run back to her village for them when the Buddha added that they had to come from a house where no death had occurred. Back in her village, although all gladly offered her the seeds, death was known in every house. Finally, late in the evening, dead-tired and with dragging feet but the dear burden still in her arms, she came back to the Buddha. There, kneeling in front of him, she laid her dead child down at his feet. 'I have understood the All-Compassionate One's teaching – I am not alone in my pain.' And though her tears were still running, they were no longer those of bitter anguish. At that, the Buddha reached out and gently touched her bent head, and there were tears in his eyes, too, as he nodded.

Grief, too, is our common human lot. Awareness of the pity of it lifts us out of the personal which is unbearable and bitter, into what is common to us all and to which the human heart responds with the releasing warmth of compassion.

We all carry a burden which we cannot lay down – it need not be a loss or grief, perhaps some unrealistic want, some resentment or aversion, an unfulfilled and unfulfillable ambition, some notion or other that seems dearer than life. The story of Kisa Gotami points at the laying down of this burden, but also tells us that this is not possible by just an act of will and that only utter exertion to the point of exhaustion makes it possible to let go, lay it down or offer it up, reverently, to some ultimate value greater than or above 'I'.

What does ultimate value mean? And yes, of course I want to lay down my burden, get rid of it. Trouble is that however much I want to, seemingly I cannot do so. So often this is the case: I want to yet cannot. The question then arises, do I really want to? Yes, yes! Why then can't I? This is where the ultimate value comes in which by definition is more than I. With that enters a suspicion, so unexpected and unpalatable that I do not want to air it, or look at it: this my burden that I so long to get rid of but cannot shed, could it perhaps just be I myself! And that I and my burden are one? And what is needful is a value over and above myself before which I quite naturally bow, lay myself down – and touched by which the heart opens of itself.

The simplicity of Great Faith also effects such an opening, but for most of us today this access road is no longer viable, we no longer have the simple faith of a child. What, however, is possible is to dimly intuit, for example, that the sincere believer in and by an act of worship may feel touched by a Divine Presence; and at being so touched I and my burden melt away, which is experienced as a state of grace.

There is, however, a real danger in such close encounters: if I am not meek, no longer in the state of the little child, should the Divine break in for one reason or another, it usually presents first its demonic face. Hence the 'Fear not' with which a heavenly messenger announces himself and which makes contact possible. The awe and fear evoked by the ultimately unknown and unknowable, the 'totally other' as Rudolf Otto called it, shatters by its tremendous power and may swallow 'I'– total ecstasy to the point of Dyonisian madness or possession, temporal or permanent.

All developed religions are well aware of that danger and have evolved ways of training. One could think of them also as ways of approach to suitably prepare the practitioner so that the melting into oneness may take place as a happening of grace.

Primitive societies have their shamans and priests to lead periodic enactments of their mythology and so the community is ritually purged of the demonic. Such ceremonies are always public whereas the truly religious way of transcendence is individual; in primitive societies only the shaman goes a lonely way along which he gains his power.

The various New Age trends extol primitive societies and, indeed, seem to have much in common with them but only at first glance. For the psyche of a so-called primitive, if he still exists as such, and the psyche of a disillusioned, opted out, late twentieth century Westerner, though their line and reach of vision is about the same, their 'ken', how they picture what they perceive, is not. They do not differ in essence but in how they see, perceive and in their corresponding reactions. So it is not surprising to find in the New Age Movement a disposition towards the supernatural, with a good deal of the downright demonic/satanic, and a great interest in 'alternative methods' from healing to dowsing, crystals to stars, all having in common that these are 'naturally' in oneself and need little if any learning – at the most a charismatic guru. Unsurprisingly, all are of an almost hysterical emotionality which also fits in well with the secular demand of 'my rights' as well as my demands for compensation in case of anything having gone wrong.

Which brings us back to the story of Kisa Gotami, for whom everything had gone devastatingly wrong. She had nothing left in the world, only the burden of her dead child.

In the course of these stories we will frequently come across the place where nothing is left. This place, not being a physical locality, metaphorically exemplifies the state where 'I' is prepared, ready, meek enough for a 'break-in' of the Transcendental/Divine. This transformation happens of its own accord, in its own time, when conditions are ripe, and can neither be produced nor hindered by intention. But the way towards it, and how it is approached, is the subject of most of these stories. All ways to it are in a way only One Way, from I to 'No-I'; but the manifold ways differ as to religious formulations, and even more so as to individual application and perceptions.

To me, my burden seems different from yours but we all want to get rid of it. The purpose of such parables then is that, whether we are conscious of our search or just because the beloved burden is too great to bear, one or the other of these stories may click in and, however dimly, point a direction, and/or bring hope. With it may arise the will and strength to set out on the great endeavour which is also called the Great Way. By our actually walking it, the obstacle 'I' is worn away until there is 'so little left' that the portals of the kingdom that is within open of themselves, and another heir has entered one of his father's many mansions.

A true letting go of one's very own beloved burden effects a complete transformation. All religions aim at such transformation, but in more personal terms, it results in a joyous, unselfish, warm-hearted humaneness that now functions freely in ordinary daily life.

The way towards it is pointed out by this moving story of Kisa Gotami – but we ourselves need to walk it with our own feet, and as dauntlessly as she did, before we too come to the 'no-place' where there is 'so little left' that suddenly, by the touch of the Buddha's bliss-bestowing hand, we behold and realize our own True Face.

2 *The Parable of the Poisoned Arrow*

It is as if a man had been wounded by an arrow thickly smeared with poison and his friends were to procure for him a physician; and the sick man were to say, 'I will not have this arrow removed until I have learnt who the man was who shot it, of which caste he was, from which village, from which tree his bow was made, from which his arrow, from where the poison on the arrow...' That man would die before he had found out all he sought.

'How obvious', we think, and 'how simple people were long ago.' Yet in our enlightened age, we do just the same! We wish to find out and to know the causes and ramifications before we let ourselves do something. Side-tracked from doing what is necessary in the situation by stupidity, cowardice or fear, we seek to escape from unpleasantness or from a painful task. CG Jung once likened such tactics to a man who in the dead of night hears a suspicious noise in the basement and rushes up to the attic to see whether a burglar has broken in!

We all play such evasive games in our commonplace, ordinary circumstances. It is wonderful how busy we can get and keep ourselves when faced with the need to reply to a difficult letter or any other unpalatable task. Stress symptoms arise perhaps as much from not wanting to face it than from being overworked; even the latter might be escapism. This is why we never become acquainted with our emotional framework, only try to hold at bay its obvious excuses or to avoid them altogether by repression. We know this latter to be unwholesome to say the least. Nevertheless, all too easily we are swept away by some emotional eruption and then resort to deceiving ourselves by some deflective action like looking for the burglar in the attic. This metaphor has even deeper meaning in the light of our story: we fabricate a host of seemingly reasonable questions and thus effectively avoid responding to what is required here and now.

Our parable puts this bluntly: the man dies in consequence of avoiding the main issue – the poisoned arrow in his arm. And since these parables explicitly pinpoint attitudes, what does that exemplify?

The shock and pain of being hit by an arrow, poisoned or otherwise, is considerable. The consequent task of having to endure its being wrenched or cut out of the quivering flesh and the wound cleaned, is a formidable requirement. A certain amount of adrenaline, purveyor of precious energy, is released to that purpose – correct response equals survival! What a pity then to fritter it away in idle and unhelpful enquiries instead of acting while the energy lasts and the poison has not yet spread throughout the body. Hence the all-importance of the task in hand, here and now. Do we always give ourselves to it as the situation requires, smoothly and without fuss? The energy for it is at hand unless, misguided by my emotional responses and assumptions in a given situation, I get carried away. It cannot be stressed too much that it is my emotional responses that misdirect the energy and thus cause it to rush up into the well-grooved tracks of aversion or aggression originating from sticky attachments.

But do we attend to the given task? In all our doing? How much are we really here and now, and how much 'away', daydreaming or chasing some train of irrelevant thought, planning some course of action, diverting ourselves from what we are actually doing? This grows on us more and more until we no longer can relax with ourselves and need constant distractions from here and now. Hence our addiction to telephone, television, radio, car radio, car phone, home computer, drugs, 'raves' and the rest.

Yet the satisfaction of a good job well done derives from the smooth flowing with the action/energy. This then is the reward of having been given into and become at one with the job in hand – whether washing up or conducting a symphony, etc. Thus the energy flow, unless kept collected and exercised, dries up and atrophies and with it the sap goes out of life. Hence one of today's problems especially assailing young people is their seeming to have little energy, as if the stuffing had gone out of them; or conversely being haplessly ridden by raw energy, lashed on by it into hotly pursuing some well-meaning but ill-considered ideal blown up out of all proportion by that same energy which in effect is the blind drive motivated by my/our advantage/conviction only.

So we fall by the wayside, opt out, have nervous breakdowns or even go to prison. When eventually we arrive at the age of retirement, we are utterly unprepared for it. Statistics indicate early deaths; with the breakdown of the family, the dreaded old-age home is our lot. There, without much interest but with much unhappiness, we vegetate until death releases us.

All because we will not face this moment here and now, and the task of it – whatever that task might be! Why do we so avoid it, as if we were frightened of it? Or are we so frightened?

Zen Masters encourage us to 'Look at the place where your feet stand'. Convinced we know that anyway, we want to get away from it to somewhere better or more interesting. But do we really know that place? Can we pause in our heedless rush and stand still? Just for a moment! Catch the breath and look – then what?

It seems unbearable; nothing to do, no distractions. I label it as downright moronic! A fear creeps up – and I turn away – anything is better than that! But just experiment, endure for a while, do not even try to push it away – just let it be. Without being fed by attention, things will die down and become quiet. We are new to this inner quiet nowadays, have even begun to fear it. But our acceptance makes it come alive, a presence which widens out and pervades all activities – which are now simply responses to the given situation without any pressure; and as that each act in itself is also wholly rewarding.

We can try this out, experiment with it; but there must be the determination to bear and sit out the inner clamouring until it fades into silence. Needless to say, such endurance inevitably acquaints us with our raw emotions – which we seek to avoid; yet the energy to 'stay the course' derives from just this endurance.

And what can we make of the arrow? The great lesson is perhaps not to see it as misfortune that has befallen me, but as a means to stop me in my headlong rush and thus opening up just such an opportunity! If we could look at any misfortune in this positive way, we cannot but grow in human stature and warmth of heart. Nor is this particularly Eastern, for in our tradition, too, is the story of the 'wounded healer'.

So perhaps when next we find ourselves pursuing a long line of inquiry, we might pause for a moment and ask ourselves what we really and concretely want to find out? Or what we are running away from? If we are courageous, we may stumble on to the adventure of our life.

3 *The Pleasant Downy Creeper*

It is as if in the last month of the hot season, a creeper's seed pod should burst and a seed of the creeper should fall at the root of a Sal tree. Then the spirit residing in that Sal tree, afraid and agitated, might fall atrembling. Then the friends and acquaintances, the kith and kin of that spirit who resides in the Sal tree – the spirits of parks, of groves, of trees, residing in medicinal herbs, in grasses and woods – gathering together might give comfort thus, 'Do not be afraid, for a peacock might swallow this seed, or a deer might eat it, or a forest fire might burn it, or workers in the wood might remove it, or white ants might eat it, or it might not germinate.'

Yet, if none of these happened, then it might indeed germinate. Rained on heavily by the monsoon clouds, it might grow apace, and a young, soft and downy creeper, clinging to it, might fasten on to the Sal tree.

Then it might occur to the spirit residing in the Sal tree, 'Why did these worthy friends and acquaintances, seeing the future peril in this creeper's seed, comfort me and advise me not to be afraid, for chances were that it would not germinate? Very pleasant is the touch of this young, soft, downy and clinging creeper.' But the creeper in time covers the Sal tree; when it has covered it, it might form a canopy above it, it might produce dense undergrowth, eventually dangling down to the ground: a matted thicket, which might strangle every great branch of the Sal tree.

Then it might occur to the spirit residing in the Sal tree, 'It was because of seeing this future peril in the creeper's seed that those worthy friends comforted me, saying it might not germinate. For now, because of this creeper's seed I am suffering sharp and acute pain'.

We all recognize ourselves in this parable – and on first sight it does not seem to need a commentary at all. But as usual, there are hidden subtleties which we do well to dig out and consider. Just that is the value of these parables, that they portray what is obvious but also what is hidden beneath the obvious and not easily accessible to the deluded 'I' that notoriously looks 'the other way'.

So there is the Sal tree. Sal trees are very special in Buddhist stories; it is under a pair of them that the Buddha laid himself down and died, that is he entered final Nirvana, not to be reborn again. In Buddhism, rebirth, so-called, is what is feared, the eternal round of suffering, whirling on and on, bound on the wheel of change without release. So perhaps the Sal tree spells out the possibility of deliverance by 'waking up' and 'heedful striving on' as the dying Buddha exhorted his sorrowing disciples.

Our so-called age of enlightenment sees nature as being dead and to be freely exploited. Once nature was seen as animate, a goddess, the Great Mother, and all she brought forth was 'of her nature', obviously alive. So, what the Greeks call a tree dryad, the spirit of the Sal tree, is a minor deva, a heavenly being of the vegetable kingdom who inhabits the tree. Its life is the tree's and it dies with the tree. If that perception were still alive, the mantle of divinity would be seen spread wide and brother stone and sister flower, together with you and I, would be one vast community. Tree-felling is a most serious, sacred business; the devata must be warned about it in good time so that a new home can be arranged and rituals of placation enacted. With nature thus alive, greediness is out – and we would have no problem about dwindling rainforests!

Anyway, the devata/dryad/semi-divine spirit of this particular Sal tree is disturbed and afraid. It sees the seed of the creeper, knows it for what it is, but bound to its tree cannot do anything about this tiny threat! All it can do is tremble!

And seeing it thus tremble, all the other nature spirits around it try to comfort it with soothing talk that after all 'there is many a slip between a cup and a lip', and the dread thing might not happen after all! And yes, how we try to cheer up a friend in trouble, try to talk him out of it, or at least distract him from his worries, 'If I were you ... !' It is easy to talk thus, for I am not you and do not have your trouble, worry, pain – nor do I know what I would do if factually I were in your situation.

Real compassion never attempts to gloss over a serious misfortune. Just that is the difference between a friend in need and an acquaintance who, though friendly, is not really bothered when faced with my distress or sorrow. The true friend allows himself to be moved by the friend's plight, and together they may come upon a course of action or of conduct that resolves the problem.

A good test for this – either facing the dilemma that has arisen and finding a way to deal with it, or trying to forget it by heedlessly distracting oneself from it. We are doing it to ourselves too! 'I really ought to mend this, patch up that, write that letter' – but not just now, can't be bothered now, am tired, am in a bad mood anyway, thoroughly moody – must distract myself – telly, phone, newspaper, pub ... ! On my way home my keys drop through the hole in my pocket which I did not mend – and now? Back, I look frantically through all my pockets – they are gone! A locksmith is called or I force open the door which now cannot be locked. I have a sleepless night in case a thief tries to come in, and must stay home tomorrow to wait for the locksmith! 'For the want of a nail ... '. There are times when one has to go out with the hole in one's pocket – and others when one just does – but then one had better keep that hole in mind heedfully!

So in our parable the devata's anxiety is soothed by the manifold suggestions of its friends; it listens to all of them and it seems the odds are overwhelmingly against the seed ever sprouting. It is bad advice – but we are ready to be lulled by it, even if the evasion 'it may not come to pass' is not self-produced. The story of Death's Three Messengers (No. 11, pp.63–67) treats the same theme, but from the side of one's own heedlessness rather than being beguiled by friends.

But this is only the beginning of the story. For against all the fondly imagined odds, the seed does germinate as is the nature of seeds; with no mishap it grows apace and the young, soft and downy creeper attaches itself to the Sal tree, clings to it as its support! How sweet, how pleasant – so innocent and small, surely no harm could come from such a thing? Our 'Just this once – how could that matter?' 'After all, it's only human!' And then 'just this once' again, and still again. And before long, 'I have always done it, this is just my habit' and, hell bent, I persist, heedlessly!

So the creeper grows, ensnares and strangles! And the well-meaning friends who comforted rather than advised, 'Do something, stop it!', and whose compassion seemed silly in the enjoyment of being caressed by this soft, downy creeper, those friends are now seen as knowing the peril but not knowing what to do about it.

For this latter, a good friend, a guide, is required who will prescribe a course of action that is appropriate to the situation, will advise how to deal with what now is, the seed on the ground, hole in the pocket, lost nail! Should that not be possible now – no time, no nail, etc. – then deal with it without fail at the very next stage. Do not let it grow! However pleasant, frail, sweet, unimportant, or any other seemingly good reason, never mind, just bestir yourself and do not let it grow! But finally, there are also situations where nothing can be done – or cannot be done any more. This is the case of the devata in the Sal tree. He cannot leave the tree nor destroy the threatening seed – he has no choice. Or has he? He is frightened but then allows himself to be persuaded to ignore the situation, actually accepting as pleasurable the growing peril. And when rudely awakened by being all but strangled, pain and suffering are upon him already; or in an extreme case, he is facing death unprepared. But if, aware of the growing creeper, the inevitable is truly faced and accepted, without distraction or excursions into make-believe, then a ripening can and does take place, which accepts what is inevitable and goes with it.

And just this is the lesson of our parable – to do all that is possible if and while it is possible, without being sidetracked by anything, but not to forget in all this the inter-connectedness, the living spirit of the scheme of things – and to go with it trustingly, without fear. 'God helps the sailor, but steer he must himself.' This is where the awareness arises of the difference between 'giving up' and 'giving in', gracefully going with 'what is', life or death – for re-linked to the living context of what is, fear has ceased to exist, and all walking is under a cloud of grace!

4 *The Blind Men and the Elephant*

A Rajah had a number of blind men gathered together and lined up next to an elephant. 'Oh you blind ones, behold an elephant!' So each of the blind men touched and traced what was before him: the head, ear, tusk, trunk, foot, back, tail, and tuft of the tail. Then the Rajah asked, 'Have you now studied the elephant?' Each one affirmed, and was invited to describe what he had found the elephant to be like. The one who had felt the head said it was like a pot; the one who had got hold of the ear said it was like a winnowing basket. And so each described what he had taken the elephant to be like – the tusk was like a ploughshare, the one who knew only the trunk said it was a plough; the body seemed a granary, the foot a pillar, the back a mortar, the tail a pestle, and the tuft on the tail just a broom. When each one had thus described it, they began to argue and to quarrel, shouting, 'Yes, it is! No, it is not! An elephant is not that! Yes, it is like that!' and so on, till they came to fisticuffs about the matter.

And yes, we do it ourselves every day. Our views, opinions, convictions we believe to be well-founded and, being ours, we hotly defend them if they are as much as queried. But there is more to this story than that.

Have we ever realized that we can only conceive in terms of what we already know? The small child simply perceives and is then told what it is that he has perceived. Now he 'knows', can differentiate a horse from a car; then he learns the associations that go with them – the moo-cow gives milk, etc. When we grow up, we get used to further allusions, 'sweating like a horse', the sun a 'fiery ball' – and so conceptions of a particular 'way of seeing' or culture develop. But three-quarters of this type of seeing is no longer the straight 'beholding' of what is – a veil is hung between. Moreover, this persuasive veil also screens from us the fact that what is unknown is also inconceivable; what is totally 'other' than the known cannot be conceived or imagined, and as such evokes awe and wonder or fear. This fear, being uncomfortable, is then relegated to behind the curtain and we continue to fondly believe that if but shown, or explained, I will know.

This sense of awe and wonder that earlier ages still possessed has become sentimentalized or belittled as 'nothing but'. Yet as uncanny fear it may assail us in the small hours of the night or in a lonely place, and it is alive and well in our increasingly frequent fancies and phobias. A look at the Bible will inform us that in order to 'communicate', that is to be seen and/or heard, a heavenly messenger's first words will invariably be, 'Fear not'. Only then can he 'deliver' the message, can he be heard and 'known'.

But what in itself cannot be known? We shy away from such reflections – they upset our deepest convictions that everything can be rendered down to 'reason' and is 'knowable'. But there is another, intangible side, something that cannot be known and is by nature so 'totally other' as to be inconceivable; it can only be hinted at by such concepts as God, Divine Spirit, Essence, Being, Life Force. Forms as well as concepts are form-giving, render this essence perceptible which, without form, is perceived as terrifying power. Would we not be rooted to the spot, hair raised, or fall trembling on our face if the bush we are just passing burst into flame and from within this flame a voice sounded like thunder ... !

The known can never have such effect, cannot shock or move us to the depth of our being and thus open up another dimension. Hence the embargo against 'graven images' so that in our constant endeavour to render perceptible what cannot be known, the ineffable, we do not mistake the form for the essence. And yet, we cannot leave it at that; rather, to further allay our fear and awe, we then make the images even more familiar, 'in our likeness', and we all feel cosy and go on arguing and quarrelling in the fashion of these ten blind men.

'Nothing but', we say glibly of a mystery we believe we have unravelled, and are the poorer for its loss. But what has the power to stay the hand, restrain the appetites, to hold out against the wild, heedless onrush of the passions? Sweet little 'I'? Or my fond imaginings? What naive arrogance to believe I can become quite familiar with God! True, God is approachable, but best done circumspectly; not in awe and trembling perhaps but reverently as so much more than I, and handing oneself over, 'Into Thy Hands, Oh Lord, I commend my spirit'.

Then, truly, 'Not I live but Christ lives in me'! The Christ that is all love, all gentleness – but also all strength because he knows no fear.

5 *The Monkey and the Pitch Trap*

In the high mountains of the Himalayas are areas so rough that neither men nor monkeys can live there; and there are others too rough for human sustenance but inhabited by monkeys; and again there are tracts of land, level and fertile, where both men and monkeys resort. Now in these parts men set traps of pitch to catch the monkeys. And those monkeys free from folly and greed, on seeing the pitch trap, keep far away from it. But a greedy, foolish monkey comes up to the trap, handles it with one paw, and his paw sticks fast in it. Then he uses his other paw to get free only to have this one, too, stuck in the pitch. To free both paws he seizes them with one foot, and that now sticks fast. To free both paws and one foot, he lays hold of them with the other foot, and that also sticks fast. To free both paws and both feet, he lays hold of them with his muzzle, but that now sticks fast.

That monkey, thus caught in five ways, lays down and howls, a prey for the hunter to work his will upon him.

Who then is human, and who monkey? Even in the high Himalayas and other inaccessible regions we have set up our pitch traps, full of the glue of greed and we become ever more stuck fast in them, devastating what was virgin soil or forest, despoiling the oceans of the world, polluting what we touch. Although now awakening to the consequences of our deeds, we cannot stem the tide that sweeps us towards disaster. No well-meaning sentimentality can win the day, for the rot is too far advanced; drastic measures are also out. They are either ill-conceived and ineffectively aggressive or so spot on that our times would not understand and so would not stand for them and anyway who would dare to propose such measures, much less have the power – or right – to enforce them.

Yes, we stick fast in those pitch traps of greed and want, of 'more, greater, better' and try to ignore the howling that has already started – the starving dispossessed and their cynical tormentors who wax fat and strong on the diverse proceeds of their misery. Caught we are, good and proper, but who, then, is the hunter? And why can we not understand and heed the signs and change track? 'For want of a nail a shoe was lost ...' all the way to the lost Kingdom! Knowing that what is at stake is not just the survival of a rare toad but global disaster, why do we not seem to care, for surely this knowledge must cause concern? The answer to that question is spelled out in Buddhism: because of selfish, greedy attachment. But also spelled out is a way of training to be delivered from it, to one's own benefit and that of others. There are today small groups, yes, but such worldwide impending catastrophes as erosion of land, spreading deserts, change of climate, overpopulation bring famine and starvation in their wake and diseases of all kinds. Thus they threaten all mankind today, not just a small part of the world. Unless all mankind heeds the writing on the wall and ceases to continue silly monkey-fashion, it will get stuck and itself become a prey to the hunter to work his will on. And who is the hunter? Man's own greed and aggressive arrogance. For the short term gain, the short-lived satisfaction, we heedlessly ravage the earth. To make a U-turn at this junction may still be possible – but it would demand utter selflessness from us all. Only time can and will have the last word.

6 *The Ass in the Lion's Skin – 'Nay this is not a Lion's Roar'*

A certain peddler went about selling his wares, which he carried on the back of an ass. At every place he came to he would unload the ass, drape a lion's skin over him and let him loose in some field of rice or barley. Now one day the peddler set up at the gate of a village and while his dinner was cooking, draped the lion's skin over the donkey and let him loose in a field of barley. The field-watchers, seeing the lion, did not dare to approach but rushed back and announced the news. A resourceful farmer suggested that they all take up arms and, blowing conch-shells and beating drums, they went out to the field to scare away the lion. The donkey, afraid for his life because of the commotion, brayed and thus gave himself away. And the villagers now went for him and gave him a sound beating.

This story comes from the southern canon. An exact parallel to it is a saying of Zen Master Rinzai, 'Behold the puppets prancing on the stage and look behind for him who pulls the strings'. The puppets cannot but move as they are pulled, dressed up for their respective roles – donkey's skin, lion's skin, or whatever they are to represent.

And the one who pulls the strings? Well, this is where the tragic delusion begins. 'The Dao that can be named is not the true Dao'. 'Forced to name it', it has always been given the attributes of wholeness or of the Divine. It is not a thing, not anything, and is perhaps best conceived of as a force that seems to act in a bipolar manner – cyclical as constant renewal like the seasons, 'coming to be and ceasing to be', a horizontal vector; and at the same time as a vertical vector that governs growth and development. Thus change is in two directions which yet result in one, as our word 'growth' implies: birth – infant – child – youth – adult – old age – death; but also as a family, from father to son – a continuing yet ever changing and renewing chain that functions in harmony with its inherent laws which might be seen as evolution in the natural world, the laws of which are neither arbitrary nor are they 'God-given' in a literal sense, though both terms fit, in a way. The one law that governs all might be seen as the Way All Things Really Are; it functions always in the same way and yet as fits the different forms; inherent in all forms, it 'in-forms' the individual form as well as having evolved all forms, and with them itself – an ongoing process!

This understanding is also behind the Kegon teaching of 'All in One, One in All'. Its coherent harmony is expressed in the Daoist saying, 'Man obeys the laws of earth, earth obeys the laws of heaven, heaven obeys the laws of Dao, and Dao obeys its own inherent nature.' The governing and all-embracing harmony of all with all is, even as a concept, tremendous. Awareness of it and the living with it or out of this awareness, being re-linked to it consciously, amounts to individual deliverance because in it this universal law has become conscious of itself in the individual form. What a tremendous happening – and what bliss! Small wonder it is said in a scripture of the Northern Tradition of Buddhism that the earth itself thrills and trembles with joy if but one more being comes to this realization.

What then about the peddler in the story – should he be the one who pulls the strings? The absurdity of such an assumption is obvious. So then who is he, and how come he craftily wrenches things in his favour – and gets himself into trouble because of it; his donkey was beaten up badly and is now useless, crippled.

Fundamental to all schools of Buddhism is the teaching of No-I (Anatta), the realization of which is the aim of all Buddhist practice. It results in the genuine and total insight that the idea of 'I' as a separate entity is delusory and in constant conflict with what is. Hence the perennial yearning for a seemingly 'lost' paradise or golden age, trying in all manner of ways to assuage this sense of alienation and concocting the most absurd ideas of how to recapture what, in fact, has never been lost. Forced by this delusion to look outside for what seems lacking and to arrange things as I want or would like, I constantly interfere. Busily I attempt to wrench things my way, to my or our advantage, trying to manipulate and getting angry, upset, enraged, bitter and resentful if it does not work. I do not accept that things have a habit of obeying their inherent laws in spite of the would-be manipulator.

All forms are 'in-formed' by the way things really are, the natural laws. The tragic delusion is that 'I', self-centred and attached to my likings, wrongly assume that 'I am the law', the one who can and may pull the strings, and with that begins the stress, suffering, sorrow and lament. Attachment therefore is perhaps best seen not as being attached to objects, but as attachment to the wrongly assumed and untenable concept of a separate 'I'. At times when cultural and especially religious values have been lost, this may take on frightening proportions because 'I' then attempts to take on the mantle of almightiness and so regresses down the scale of cultural evolution, denying the past and its achievements including manners, courtesy, respect. This inevitably leads to increasing violence and its complement, a maudlin sentimentality that is as foreign to the great natural laws as it is weak. Both traits also emerge as fundamentalism, a movement that in its narrow rigidity grips emotionally and so is akin to mass emotion with its danger of outbreaks of hysteria and destruction.

That is what our story warns against – the crafty peddler dressing up his donkey as a lion so as to filch fodder for it from others' fields – and for a time it seems to work fine. But then, inevitably, he comes up against someone/something that shows up the makeshift for what it really is; at which the 'others' who have been duped by this swindle, emotionally erupt in the manner of a volcano and wreak their vengeance on the makeshift rather than on the perpetrator. Do we then need to wonder why even our best intentions so often miscarry?

So perhaps it might be conducive if 'I,' the perpetrator, could turn round and stop manipulating, drop makeshift deceptions, cease from 'picture-making' and from puppeteering and rather learn to declutch from the false promptings of 'I, me, mine'. In the resulting quiet, the inherent information can be heard to whisper and make itself known once more. It has a gentle, small voice and cannot be heard while on the usual headlong, heedless rush towards or from something or other! But if heard, it fills the heart with peace, strength and compassion.

7 *Excess of Zeal*

The Venerable Sona, a rich man's son, not long after he had been fully ordained as a monk, was diligently training himself. But through excess of zeal in walking meditation he lacerated his feet and the strip where he walked up and down was dabbled with blood like a butcher's slaughtering shed. Then to the Venerable Sona, as he dwelt apart in solitude, there came a train of thought like this, 'Here I am, one of those disciples of the Exalted One who dwell in earnest zeal; but my heart is not released from any outflows without clinging. Great possessions await me at home; I might employ that wealth and do good deeds with it. How if I were to return to the layman's life and do so?'

That very day the Buddha with some monks went his round from lodging to lodging and when he saw the Venerable Sona walking and his strip dabbled with blood, he asked whose place this was. Told of the zeal with which Sona had lacerated his feet so that they were bleeding, the Buddha asked Sona, 'Did you not recently come to think that as your heart is not released from the outflows without clinging, you might return home and use your wealth to do good deeds with it?' 'It is so, Lord.'

'And formerly, when still at home, were you not skilled in playing the lute?' 'Yes, Lord.' 'Then say, Sona, when your lute strings were over-taut, did your lute then give out a sound, was it fit to play upon?' 'No, Lord.' 'But when your lute strings were neither over-taut not overslack but evenly strung, did your lute then give out a sound, was it fit to play upon?' 'It was, Lord.'

'Even so, Sona, excess of zeal makes one liable to self-exaltation, while lack of zeal makes one liable to sluggishness. Wherefore do you, Sona, persist in evenness of zeal, master your faculties and make that your aim.'

And the Venerable Sona, attending to the words of the Buddha, in no long time came to realize the aim and became awakened.

So self-evident is this story that it needs no special comment. But it is not just about Bhikkhu Sona; he is every one of us. We are all capable and liable to really lash ourselves in the first fine frenzy of any enthusiasm; but when we then soon run out of steam as run out we must, and on taking stock find that after all nothing much has happened, we tend to be discouraged and veer away to something else that beckons and catches our imagination. In short, as the analogy of the lute strings relates, we begin to doubt, to hesitate, will no longer bestir ourselves or not whole-heartedly.

This is our basic human condition, caught in which we continue to 'bob up and down in the ocean of birth and death'. To win free from it, a process of learning and training is necessary. At first, a child is to attain to the learning and culture of his time, and should he be inclined to develop further, an additional learning and training needs to be undertaken to bring spiritual values to maturity. In both cases, this process of learning and training is basic, but does not come naturally to the self-willed I. Hence the necessity of an upbringing which, if neglected, makes for unhappy adulthood, with atrophying attention span and being at the mercy of emotional energy which, untrammelled, regresses to a state of barbarity.

If undergone, however, then from this process of learning and training derives an inner strength that is now capable of holding out against debilitating emotional upsurges, is capable of sustained application, and has won a certain degree of freedom and true individuality. This is the state of the adult as a responsible member of the community; with it also arises awareness of any particular talent inherent in that person (rather than fancying that 'I have' it).

Many may settle satisfactorily at this juncture. But there are others whose very nature demands a still further step on the spiritual/evolutionary ladder – and for that, the already attained strength is not enough. So a new, and now entirely voluntary cycle of learning and training has to be undertaken to further cultivate this inner strength. Where does the latter come from? From the transformation of the emotional energy that flares and erupts like a volcano in the untrained, not brought-up state which has aptly been called 'barbarism'. As with any conflagration, the result is large-scale destruction. Cultivated, however, and transformed into what is truly human, this same energy changes into the power of spiritual sublimity and in those so 're-born' being manifests itself as a deep, warm and humble humanity.

So Sona stands for all of us; the son of a rich house – as we all are. You think not? Yet we all have the good fortune of being born with a human body, rare because in spite of our disgraceful overpopulation, we are but a tiny proportion among all the creatures in existence. And only from the human state, it is said, can deliverance be reached. We are twice fortunate to be born at a time when the Buddha's teachings are still extant, for there are times where only bogus cults and fashionable creeds hold sway; we seem to be approaching such a time. Thrice fortunate we are to be born at a place where we can come into contact with his teachings. And still more fortunate that on coming in contact with them, we feel inclined to follow them. That is the greatest good fortune for – to change the metaphor and show that all religions strive to the same goal – with that we have the key to 'our father's mansion'.

Like the Venerable Sona, we may undertake a religious training which, Buddhist or otherwise, demands devotion, diligence, strength to endure and patience. These are qualities of the heart that need to be fostered, developed and nurtured until fully ripened.

Like Sona, we go at it full of enthusiasm, only to find that our feet bleed and we have nothing to show for our efforts; then arise thoughts of giving up or trying something more promising. But as no real, selfless effort, once expended, can ever get lost, just at this junction something happens that gives a nudge again. In Bhikkhu Sona's story, it is the Buddha himself, and if we like to see it so – and it is conducive to do so – we may always see it as the Buddha himself, or nature, or Life, for all Life strives, grows towards that goal. Hence it is said that one cannot do such training for oneself alone. With that realization comes then a re-dedication, where practice and goal are no longer two but have become a joyous striving on, heedfully – that is 'persisting in evenness of zeal and mastering the faculties'.

Then again, like the Venerable Sona, 'in no long time' we shall come to realize the aim and awaken.

To what? Perhaps it is useful to get as clear as we can about this term. 'Awaken as from a dream' is the usual definition and yes, dreams and our everyday reality are fundamentally different. But perhaps it could also be seen in terms of growth. An acorn, put into the ground, if it sprouts will never become an apple tree but will grow into an oak, which is different from the acorn. And the oak, 'thus come', will in time also produce acorns that grow into oak trees.

So, 'grow' really has two vectors. One is to grow 'ever again', like grass, oaks, etc. – a cyclic renewal; the other is a vertical component that grows upwards and makes for development like child into adult, and also contains a spiritual factor that individually makes for change and development and collectively acts as cultural change, affecting understanding, religious insight, etc. This imperative for growth seems to split a primordial union and compels the resulting parts to labour themselves – as does the pearl oyster with the introduced grain! No individual form escapes these growing pains, for grow it must when it would rather indulge in the inertia of matter. In the resulting evolution ever new forms appear, both material and as thought-forms or ideas. Thus within the cyclic 'ever again', as blossoms appear in spring, there is an upward/forward thrust of development and vice versa. Where to or towards what? As the ever-returning yet ever more 'conscious' forms grow towards awareness, it seems that in its forms (for without form it is 'nothing') this growth force or life force, no matter how called, may itself become conscious, aware of itself.

Thus because of its conscious awareness, although all forms are 'informed' by what is, the human state is truly special. But to fully realize this potential of conscious awareness requires much labour. The human state suffers from the delusion of experiencing I/myself as a separate, unconnected entity. When this delusion is seen through, it dissolves like a cloud. Then, what always has been becomes clearly visible.

For such awakening no mysterious agency is necessary; being already there, the laws of nature and their functioning are now seen clearly, unbiased. In my seeing, I am always the subject, the seer, and all I see is from my point of vantage, as I see it, and I cannot see more than I am. If greedy, I see all in terms of my/our profit; if ambitious, in terms of power and imbue others with the same type of seeing and acting! Yes, we are truly blind, cannot see anything other than 'I'-coloured. The root of 'I' is extremely strong and tenacious and the texts often liken it to a strangling creeper. Like a creeper, it needs to attach itself to something and hold on to it for dear life, and to sever such a creeper is not easy, for it cannot be just hacked off; enthusiastic attempts like Bhikkhu Sona's can wreak havoc, shattering rather than transforming. The creeper clings tenaciously because it cannot stand alone and so is afraid to let go. Only 'persistence in evenness of zeal' will slowly work the transformation, the awakening from the dream of having been a separate form, a creeper, to the realization of being a 'tree' all along – world tree, world-axis, Buddha-nature. Or, in a familiar Buddhist analogy, the individual wave, while it lasts, has an individual form but in itself, in its nature, is nothing but ocean and so need not fear falling back into itself where it always has been.

But this transformation needs to be genuine, complete, total – hence the Buddha's last words to 'strive on, heedfully'.

8 *On Getting Angry*

You are angry with this man, you say. What is it you are angry with? With the hair of the head or with the hair of the body, or with the nails, etc.? Or are you angry with the earth element in the hair – and the rest? Or with the element of water – or of fire – or of air in them? What is referred to by a name like Jack or Jill is only the five aggregates, six sense organs (in Buddhism, thought is also a sense organ), six sense objects, and six sense consciousnesses. With which of these are you angry?

A person who has made the above analysis is no longer swayed by anger. Folk wisdom suggests that when fired into a 'state', to count to ten before we speak or act. Hopefully during that time we catch our breath and cool down a little. The Buddhist advice goes further: not only are we bound to cool off during this lengthy analysis, but the outcome is intellectually satisfying as well – there is no such person to be angry with! Buddhism denies a personal entity and advocates seeing things as they are: perishable, not lasting; 'contingently arising and having no separate existence' is the classical definition. Our delusion or ignorance consists in taking these conglomerations to be of substance, lasting and real, and consequently suffer on finding them constantly changing. Careful analysis shows that to cling to such a shifting conglomeration, or to be furious with it, is merely silly.

This seemingly simple advice comes from a profound insight into our human make-up. For if angry or in any emotional state, sent up by the Fires, do we not often try to reason ourselves out of it by belittling or ridiculing the cause or object that sent us? All to no avail for the Fire goes on burning brightly; long thought-streams of what the other said, his offensiveness, what I should/would answer, planning a salutary put-down for the offender, digging up in memories of old and long-forgotten grievances that, rather than calm me down, only serve to keep the Fires burning merrily and prompting me to some rash action which, as soon as committed, is either regretted or leads to further difficulties. Such brooding on my grievances and resentment is contrary to the course the parable advocates. All this has nothing to do with any attempts of mine to reason, or to blame or blast somebody/something out of existence. Such attempts are bound to fail because they look at the conflict the wrong way, deluded by my self-biased reaction to a given object or circumstance. I may have a phobia about mice, but a mouse leaves you stone-cold! So what I have to deal with is my reaction, not the mouse! This is also carefully expounded in the Parable of the Poisoned Arrow (No. 2, pp.25–29). But it is not easy to face one's own state, the emotional energy which has arisen burning inside. Actually, a full flare-up cannot be faced/endured head-on, and hence the advice to carefully analyse what is deludedly seen as the cause. This lengthy analysis serves a double purpose: it is satisfying intellectually because when concluded, the object is seen as irrelevant and whatever still burns or at least smoulders can be seen as my reaction. Now already reduced or cooled down, this energy may then be faced safely and worked with for genuine transformation.

So perhaps when we next take up the cudgels to go into battle, just lower the arm, take a deep breath, pause for a moment and look! Look at the object and start the analysis – do not allow yourself to be distracted or to be carried away into some unskilful abreaction which merely squanders the working capital of the energy which has arisen. Thus this energy or power is employed and is itself the one needful thing for successfully and satisfactorily carrying through the analysis, in and by which this energy itself undergoes transformation!

9 *The Anger-eating Demon*

Once upon a time a sickly-looking, decrepit demon sat himself down upon the throne of Shakka, leader of the Heavenly Beings. These, angered and annoyed, complained and murmured, 'Just look! Look at this decrepit demon that has usurped Shakka's seat! How dare he!' Now, in proportion to their anger, annoyance and indignation, the demon grew ever more handsome, better-looking and pleasing.

Then the Heavenly Beings went to Shakka, their leader to lodge their complaint. They told him what had happened and wondered, since he grew ever more handsome the more they complained, whether he was an anger-eating demon.

So Shakka, their leader, approached the throne, sank down on his right knee, folded his hands in front of the demon and three times called out, 'Sir, your obedient servant Shakka, leader of the Heavenly Beings.' At each time the demon became more sickly and decrepit and suddenly disappeared. Shakka resumed his seat on his throne and reminded the others not to speak harsh words in anger, not to boast and be proud, but to subdue oneself and strive on heedfully.

This is still another version of the same theme as The Ass in the Lion's Skin, (No. 6, pp.39–42). The case presented in this story is the tragic mistake of an assumed 'I' that now needs to control, manipulate, know how things should be and feels impelled to set them right – according to my/our views. 'Ah love, couldst thou and I with fate conspire, would we not shatter this sorry scheme of things to bits and build it nearer to the heart's desire' (Omar Khayyam). Well, a look at history shows us that we have always attempted to meddle; and though much has been achieved along the way, things have nevertheless grown gradually worse, more complicated, more unmanageable and uncontrollable!

Thus almost imperceptibly the sickly-looking, decrepit demon 'I' sneaks up and surreptitiously settles himself on Shakka's throne. Shakka is the leader of the heavenly hosts, divinity, godhead incarnate, and as that stands for the Great Law or the Great Way itself, rendered perceptible as Shakka in this our version.

Shakka's seat, the throne of the Divine, the altar for the spirit to reside, is the human heart. Periodically, it seems, instead of worshipping at the throne of this residing or inherent divine spirit, (Christ, Buddha-nature), we deluded beings attach ourselves to false gods somewhere outside. When the spirit in the heart gets neglected it leaves this altar to stage self-portraits outside, and on to the empty throne now sneaks up – nature abhors a vacuum – a 'sickly-looking, decrepit demon'. Do we recognize in this description our 'godlike image' of 'I'? Our frantic dance around the golden calf of the moment? Not we, blinded and deluded as we are!

In the story, the Heavenly Beings are wise to this stealthy manoeuvre at once, but themselves being weak, only complain angrily at such brazen daring. Boosted by such a show of ineffectual weakness and coming to believe in his own power and almightiness, the usurper waxes, blows himself up, and actually begins to look the part.

Now, Heavenly Beings do not use force, but they have their own ways of redressing the balance – 'the mills of God grind slowly, but they grind exceeding fine.' So they now sought out Shakka and told him what had happened, also confessing that their own anger at seeing this decrepit thing on his, Shakka's, throne, far from ousting him ashamed, only had made him look ever more sleek and handsome like a cream-fed cat! Could their anger have been the cream he battened on?

Then Shakka, divinity incarnate, approached his own throne and there – it is hardly conceivable, is it? – sank down on his right knee and raising folded hands three times in succession announced himself with meticulous politeness, faultless address, 'Sir, your obedient servant, Shakka, leader of Heavenly Beings.' Truly cultivated good form holds under all circumstances and in all situations alike, even under greatest provocation. And it may evoke or effect surprising reactions. Anyway, each time the demon shrank, became more sickly and decrepit and then disappeared suddenly – gone back to the nothing from which he had manifested.

Upon which Shakka resumed his throne – in the human heart we may take it, and reminded the others, the faculties of perception, of conduct and of awareness, all of them spirit-related, not to be beguiled into wrong action and unbecoming conduct, not to speak harsh words in anger, not to boast and be proud, but to subdue all self-deceit and to strive on heed-fully. Which, incidentally, is also the answer to the perennial question, 'But if nothing is done about it, what then?' Does the demon then wax limitless? Shakka, the Divine, shows the Way. All that waxes too big works its own demise – which is also a facet of that Great Law of the Way All Things Really Are.

10 *The Bare Bones*

There was a young novice living in a country temple. One evening a merchant and his entourage arrived seeking shelter for the night. Among their group was the merchant's beautiful young daughter. The novice fell in love at first sight. That night he could not sleep. He was torn between his life in the temple and his love for the merchant's daughter.

Early the next morning he went to see the abbot and asked permission to go and work for the merchant in the city. He hoped that he might eventually win the love of the merchant's daughter. The abbot consented. The merchant gladly accepted the boy and over the next few years he rose from general messenger to chief clerk. At the same time he also succeeded in winning the daughter's heart and with the merchant's blessing they were married. They were both very happy. Soon they had a beautiful baby boy. A few years later the merchant retired and handed over the business to his son-in-law who proved more than adequate and business thrived. Shortly afterwards the old merchant became ill and died. His widow followed just a few months later. For a while the young couple were very sad but their love for each other and their son helped them through and happiness returned.

As the years passed they continued to be blissfully happy and the business flourished. But tragedy struck when a horse pulling a heavily laden cart shied and backed away, rolling the cart over the son as he played in the courtyard. The boy died, leaving the couple torn with grief. Eventually, however, time and their love for each other healed their grief, and soon the wife was expecting another child. They were both once again very happy and business continued to flourish.

But misfortune struck again. The wife and unborn baby both died during childbirth. He was utterly devastated. At the same time the whole country was going through a very difficult time and his business began to decline. Eventually he had to sell all he had in order to pay off his debts. He was penniless, homeless and heartbroken. In a daze he started to walk. Five days later he found himself along a dusty country road that somehow seemed familiar. On reaching a crossroads he instinctively took a left turn. After a short distance he came to a small path and there ahead stood the temple where as a boy he had been a novice. Tears filled his eyes. He approached the temple gate and knocked. A young novice hurried out and welcomed him. He said he had been on the road for several days and asked if he could shelter there for the night. Inwardly he hoped that he might be able to see the old abbot once again, but, as he talked to the novice on the way in, he discovered that his old teacher had in fact died several years earlier.

That night he lay awake reviewing his life. How as a young boy he had left the temple in search of love and happiness. How he had found both, and for many years had lived a blissful life with everything he could wish for. And how, eventually, the march of time had taken all this away from him.

With deep sadness he realized the futility of searching for happiness within the changing conditions of this life and realized the importance of following the religious way. He wished he had stayed at the temple and longed to see the old abbot who had been like a father to him. Pondering in this way, regret gave way to hope, and he vowed that the very next morning he would ask the new abbot if he could stay on, ragged and dishevelled though he was, and help around the temple.

Having reached this resolve, the cares of the last few years seemed to fall away and he fell into a deep and peaceful sleep. He was woken early the next morning by the sound of horses and people in the temple courtyard. Rushing to the window he saw the merchant and his retinue setting off on the final stage of their journey back to the city.

He watched in silence, and then, with tears of gratitude rolling down his cheeks he walked quietly to the shrine room, bowed reverently before the altar, and gave thanks to the Lord Buddha.

He remained in the temple for the rest of his life, first serving the old abbot, and then succeeding him as incumbent.

In a way, this story needs no comment at all; the meaning is perfectly clear; do not chase after happiness in this changeable world. But people do and why not? Yet we all know the harrowing grief of sudden loss, the bitter frustration of betrayal, the anguish of unrequited love – this is the story to look at then. Sorrow and lament are the regular accompaniments of life, are what is grave and constant in human experience. These days we are little prepared for their emergence, and so have nothing to counter or hold out against them or to endure them when they befall us.

But there is still another message in this story, and a very important one, which we may ponder to advantage. Whether we like it or not, nature is eclectic and hieratic. In the teeming multitude of sentient beings there is nevertheless an inherent order, a structure that allots the individuals their place as well as their meaning. In this meaningfulness there is no better or worse; important for us conscious sentient beings is that this meaning is realized and lived to its full potential; that constitutes happiness – not the amassment of riches, or the top of the ladder. So the message is about vocation. Here, the dreamer is a novice, not just any young boy. And for him, with a religious vocation, even a fulfilled life as the dream showed him, has in the long run no meaning; it glides away and after a period of suffering he returns to where he belongs.

Two opposing opinions have always held sway in us conscious sentient beings – the two principles of light and dark that make up our world.

For small bands of roaming nomads, and even in small settled villages, then and now, the only division of labour is that of sex. With the emergence of the earliest city states went a division of labour made necessary by the requirements of a larger number of people living together at close quarters. Masons and tanners and weavers, scribes and priests, crafts, professions, vocations came into being – and since then also the tug of war between predestination and free will. This is a dangerous subject to air, and it has been misunderstood or intentionally misinterpreted so often that it is all but discredited. Yet behind it is a message that might well spell out a remarkably constructive and rewarding solution if those two seeming opposites are seen not as two but as an harmonious one. How can that be? Our story points at it.

Exemplified even in our day is the fact that talents are unevenly distributed. But even great talent needs dedicated application to blossom, demands devoted and painstaking work all the way; without talent, with the same effort put in, a certain competence may be acquired, but spark and spirit will be missing. The great conductor, violinist, or composer is a good example even in our days of assumed equality. We also see a trend nowadays to the arts and crafts such as pottery or weaving, etc. Not surprising, for doing and shaping with one's hands brings a satisfaction we have almost forgotten in our heady rush for more of whatever we imagine will, once possessed, satisfy for good.

In this pursuit we have forgotten the danger of one-sidedness – either of rigid enforcement or preordainment as exemplified in a class system that has no loopholes; or in a chaotic, structureless, levelling down to the lowest denominator of all being the same. Although we all are human beings, we differ individually from each other. Already born with specific bodies and dispositions we later diversify still further. Three or more children, born in the same family, brought up by the same parents under the same circumstances, right from infancy will show different traits. The one-time fashionable excuse of blaming it all on parents or environment just holds no water.

And so we see in the long course of history that a real talent, a true inclination, will always persevere and will come to the surface against all odds and as such be accepted by the environment which itself benefits by its artists, artisans, craftsmen, mathematicians, priests or whatever. To go against or be forced against such overwhelming inclination impoverishes both the community and the individual. And in the absence of such a pronounced vocation, the seemingly 'given' trade or profession may be made 'one's own' and so yield satisfaction for the thus engaged individual and be of use to the community. The latter is the easier because less demanding. The former demands constant and wholehearted, not to say selfless, dedication which is the meaning of 'vocation', and if it is gainsaid by the individual, will be productive of much unhappiness.

In our story, the young man is already a novice in a temple; this is his true vocation. The latter is always 'tested' so as to be reaffirmed and thus become more and more conscious. The myths of all times and cultures stress this, and so both warn and prepare the individual for this 'passage'. The factual answer to the demand, 'Why can't I be a Beethoven', or a Shakespeare, or a Karajan, is simply, 'Because I am not'.

Thereby hangs yet a further issue. Though I may not be aware of it, or may not like it, factually we all are bound within the limits of a situation; no one lives in a vacuum. We are creatures of the last decades of the twentieth century, inheriting the bare remnants of a Western culture-continuum with all that implies and we are willy-nilly impregnated by current trends as well as by personal and individual circumstances. But though we cannot repudiate these circumstances for they are 'us', within these boundaries we are free – at least still here in the West but actually always; what we are not free of is the consequences of our decisions and actions within the given binding circumstances. Thus, should we not like our job, boss, family, or whatnot, we are free to march out on them right here and now; but this will inevitably entail consequences. Should these consequences be unacceptable, we choose to remain where we are – and actually this is exactly what we do. And so, wondrously, though we do not realize it, but actually, factually, since we cannot oversee the limitation of the circumstances for our world as it is with night and day, light and dark, this our time now – within these limits we are, each of us, exactly at the place where we most wish to be or we would not be there! 'But it is only duty that holds me here', I cry. Well, so duty is what means most to me and still I am at the place/position I most want to be, everything else being not acceptable or not preferable. And with the dawning of that realization, with that awareness, I can then settle down and know that what puts me under stress, tenses me, makes me feel unsatisfied or unreasonably demanding is I myself, my delusion of wanting to be something other than what I am!

But it does not stop there, either. Because once the realization has arisen that I am as I am, there is then also the possibility of change – change by truly accepting what I am and making good of it: either a satisfactory and rewarding life with job and family, or accepting a given vocation. The latter may often go against momentary inclinations or infatuations or fashionable trends, but if lived obediently even if not meeting acclaim by others, also spells out a satisfactory and rewarding life.

Which means that the shouter, the one who wants to be acclaimed, the one who wants compensation, demands 'my' right, is the unhappy one who has never found his place or vocation and now needs others to affirm something that is a mere nothing – and needs it so desperately that the demands for acclaim, following, affirmation, are ever more voracious because, being illusory, they must remain unfulfilled.

And so at the end of the story – life always being satisfying even at its worst – there is the happy ending: the merchant, good family man and successful in business yet without being aggressive and so without the constant strain of one-upmanship, thus in comfortable circumstances and radiating these among his family and servants, is in his own place and those around him also profit by it. The merchant and his train depart. The novice, equally grateful at having woken up from his temporary infatuation and having his true vocation affirmed, is now ready to further effort along the spiritual way.

And the great lesson to be learned is, both are happy; both are right, each in their own way, as it fits them. The merchant is a pious man as befits his station and happiness; he puts up at the temple. He does not hanker after the spiritual life; he is a merchant, and fulfilled as that. And the novice now no longer hankers after the worldly life with its pleasures and vicissitudes; they have lost their attraction and so he can settle down and continue to grow spiritually.

Each is how and what he is and satisfied with that; both right, none better, none worse. That is the real lesson, the tremendous lesson that is so very difficult to learn while my very thinking is a value-process of picking and choosing – of what is better and what is worse, what more pleasant and what less, right and wrong. To see the sameness in differentiation and differentiation in sameness makes for the clear seeing that the Buddha advocates, for it allows the others to be what they are, to fulfil their potential without the childish demand that they 'ought to be' what I think they are because that assumption severs the common bond between us – which severing is the beginning of aggression and enmity.

Yet such 'clear seeing' does not blind against perception of basic right and wrong; only the latter, now seen clearly, is not to be fought against but rather demands a steadfast holding to the basic human decencies. Clear seeing is looking without heat, without the optical delusions produced by the Fires. From the viewpoint of the basic sameness that unites us all, clearly seeing means beholding both our differences and enjoying the diversity of life, as well as clearly differentiating right from wrong, Buddha from Mara. This then makes possible to hold out against the latter, not taking hot-headed issue with it. The latter, in its opinionatedness only adds to the existing forces of darkness.

Hamlet's question, therefore, might be answered in the affirmative: 'TO BE' and, thus being, to come ever closer to what we are. Thus we come to fulfil our potential as well as what life itself wants us to do – which gives meaning and purpose to the individual life, tying it into the larger context of life itself. Only then is there true satisfaction and fulfilment, making good of our birthright. And, incidentally, assisting others to fulfil theirs.

11 *Death's Three Messengers*

On his wedding day the groom was taken away and brought before Yama, judge and ruler of the dead. The young man bitterly complained; so young, quite unprepared, and on his wedding day, too! Was this fair, was this just? Without any warning whatsoever – out of the blue! Yama was moved by the young man's plight and sent him back to life, also promising to send three messengers so that he would be warned in time and could prepare himself.

Sixty years went by. Sadly to say, the man who had been heedless in his youth continued thus heedlessly, and when again brought before Yama, complained as of old. Yama asked why he had not heeded the messengers he had sent as promised. 'What messengers – no, no messenger came to me.' Yama questioned him more closely, 'O man! Did you not see the first of death's messengers visibly appear among men?' 'Lord, I did not.' And Yama said, 'Did you not see among all the people a woman or a man, eighty or ninety years of age, decrepit, crooked as the curved rafter of a gable roof, bowed down, leaning on a staff, tottering along, with youth long fled, broken-toothed, and blotched with freckles?' 'Lord, I did.' And Yama asked, 'O man, did it not occur to you, being a person of mature intelligence and years, that you also are subject to old age, in no way exempt, and resolve to henceforth act nobly with body, speech and thought?' And the man replied, 'Lord, I did not think.'

Then Yama asked him if he had not seen the second of death's messengers, and again the man said he had not. King Yama then said, 'O man! Did you not see among all the people men or women, diseased, suffering, grievously sick, rolling in their own filth, who when lying down had to be lifted up by others, and by others had to be laid down again?' He replied, 'Lord, I did.' Yama asked, 'Did it not occur to you, being a person of mature intelligence and years, that you, too, are subject to disease and in no way exempt, and to resolve henceforward to act nobly with body, speech and thought?' 'Lord, I did not think', responded the hapless one again.

A third time King Yama questioned him, 'Did you not see the third of death's messengers visibly appear among men?' 'Lord, I did not.' And Yama said, 'Did you never see a man or woman that had been one day dead, or two days dead, or three days dead, and had become swollen, black, and putrid?' 'Lord, I did.' 'And did it not occur to you that you, too, are subject to death and in no way exempt, and to resolve henceforth to act nobly with body, speech and thought?' And again the man answered, 'Lord, I did not think.' And Yama addressed him, 'O man! Through thoughtlessness you failed to see the messengers. Through thoughtlessness you failed to act nobly with body, speech and thought. Yours is the action, you alone shall feel the consequences.'

Surely this story is so explicit that it needs no comment – anything added to it would be as needless as trying to paint legs on a snake to make it walk. And yet implicit in it is a question that begs to be answered, for it is at the very bottom of our dilemma, of our own problems and whatever we have made to go wrong with our world.

Our young man was forewarned – had actually stood in front of death and been granted a remission. He knew that it was fact and not just imagination and that he would have to face it again and account for himself, be ready to do so and yet, 'Oh Lord, I did not think'. And so the question that poses itself is how it is possible that in spite of us knowing the consequences, in spite of knowing 'the voice of conscience' and its guiding, in spite of actually ourselves mostly willing to do what is right and good, yet we forget, fail to bring it off? What is it that deters us against our own understanding, against our own better wishes and inclination? What is the obstacle in ourselves – for there it is to be found, not blamed on outside circumstances that prevent 'poor, innocent me' who in the heat of the moment 'forgot'.

Not only Buddhist teachings try to answer this question – all religions in their own ways address it and offer their own solutions to this the perennial dilemma that has accompanied us human beings from the beginning. In Christianity it is called original sin and in Buddhism the basic delusion, an opaqueness that dims sight as does turbid water. We, having never known anything but this opaqueness, have no means to detect its existence, so need to be taught of another state and then strive towards it. Or, in another frequently used analogy, we are like a dreamer whose dream, however absurd or nightmarish, nonetheless seems utterly real but who, once awoken from it, realizes with heartfelt relief that he bears no traces of just having been mauled by a tiger!

We cling to this opaque world as the only one we know. We constantly hurt ourselves, bumping against other objects in this murkiness, trying to shove things out of our way or to arrange them to be more convenient, pleasing, and profitable for me. Thus we keep ourselves busy and complaining with nothing much ever achieved. For although we have shifted some of the obstructions, others have sprung up in their place and for every seeming advantage gained another obstacle has emerged. So we still carry on shifting and complaining.

Or we may take to heart the perennial teachings of there being another state, other than our customary murkiness and actually strive along a suggested route or course of action. Since this is likely to be quite different from my customary activities and preoccupations, and often flatly goes against them as well as contradicts some of my favourite views and opinions, the going is notoriously hard.

Long since schooled to find good excuses for not doing what I do not want to do, I might now busy myself with good works and pious deeds – going through the motions of doing good without letting it go more than at most skin-deep. Nothing will then change. Or else I allow myself to be diverted by some appetising morsel – and there are always plenty about – and succeed in getting so distracted that, to my own detriment, I cleanly forget all about there being a state where clear seeing obtains. For when the eternal verities stare me in the face, when sickness, old age and death confront me, what then? The messengers I have ignored, the teachings I have not followed, and heedless in the pursuit of my ideas I have noticed nothing, 'I forgot, Lord'. Thus arise bitterness and resentment against the inexorable 'workings of fate', 'Karma', the all-pervading law governing sowing and reaping.

Against this stands the Buddha's final message, almost a plea from the depth of his compassion for us deluded, suffering beings who cause so much pain to ourselves as well as to others, 'Impermanent are all compounded things – strive on heedfully.'

12 *The Forest Dweller*

Once more the Buddha had come to stay in the Bamboo Grove near Rajagriha, and Mahakasyapa, who was dwelling in a forest hermitage, came to pay his respects to him. Both had grown old together, and the Buddha, seeing Mahakasyapa in his coarse, rough garments, said, 'You are grown old, Mahakasyapa. Burdensome are these coarse, cast-off patchwork robes. Take it easier, get softer robes, allow yourself to be invited for meals by laymen, and take up your abode with me.' But Mahakasyapa asked permission to continue as he was, dwelling by himself in the forest, rag-robed, living on alms, contented and loving solitude. This life that he had lived for so long and that fitted him as his old robes did, he now had his comfort in and was well content.

The same, yet not the same – how difficult to see this in depth. Two boys, same parents, brought up in the same home – yet they are quite different. No two cats are alike. But there is also an overall way – that of the adult of a given species, group, culture and which has to be 'learned'. Without such learning, continuity is threatened, 'goes to pieces' and 'breaks up'. True development always rests securely on what was and grows forward/upward from there. Treetops are on top of trees; they do not float in mid-air!

Nowadays a general resistance is felt against this basic growth/learning and yet, only out of this can a communal 'new' develop – when a sufficient number of individuals, having realized the 'norm', now can develop their own individual line and are free to do so. To follow our promptings towards a specific vocation is safe only after having realized the norm, when it 'becomes clear'. True, there are child prodigies – but that is the exception rather than the rule. The extrovert boy, excelling in sport, may devote his life to it; but, should he no longer be able to continue, having been brought up to the norm, he has the whole field of his culture to choose from, and will have a rewarding 'second life'. Whereas his brother, sensitive and almost timorous, was strengthened by means of cultivating the norm and may then go into a job or profession where just his sensibility and tact are his advantage. Moreover, even if we have to earn a living that is not exactly in line with our own gifts and talents, having been brought up to the norm means that there is much that can be developed and cultivated further as our hobbies. The resulting interest and dedication will hold also in the face of difficulties and problems because such pursuits produce an inner contentedness that knows no envy, has no demands and finds its joy in what is.

A remarkable man, Mahakasyapa, yes; but also a man, a human being as we all are. And we all can become as Mahakasyapa – if we sufficiently bestir ourselves.

13 *A Life free from Passion is not Bland*

King Milinda asked the Venerable Nagasena, 'What is the difference between one who has passion and one who is free from passion?'

'The one clings, the other does not cling.'

'What do you mean by clings and does not cling?'

'The one covets, the other does not covet.'

'But as I see it, both he who has passion and he who is free from passion have the same wish, that, whether hard or soft, his food should be good; neither wishes for what is bad.'

'He who is not free from passion experiences both the taste of that food and also passion due to that taste; while he who is free from passion experiences the taste of that food, but not passion due to that taste.'

Who would not wish to get beyond all the stress and tension, the worries and problems that beset our daily lives – to be free of all the dross and trivia that accompany it? So we might be inclined to follow the Buddha's Way that proclaims just this deliverance. But hardly have we engaged to do so when it appears not to be as straightforward as it seemed; rather than somehow making it all happen for me, it asks me to actively apply myself. And if we then have our feet on the path, soon another spectre threatens and this is the subject of our story.

For though I want to get rid of what I do not like because it irks or hurts, I do not want to give up what I like, my habits, what I always did or had, my notions, ideas, opinions and convictions, the way it suits me; all these are dear to me, belong to me, in fact are me. Even changing my meal times – why should I? What for? We can experiment: just for two weeks we determine to get up ten minutes earlier than usual; for no reason at all, no benefit in health or spiritual stature, just to see whether we can bring it off. No need to argue the point, just try and find out. From the third day on all kinds of reactions will arise – anger and frustration erupt, querying what good this is to anybody, likely to end up as a soulless automaton! In fact we are concocting excuses to reason it away as simply not worth any effort! Well, just that is clinging to my way; and the frustration and anger that well up at my way being crossed or thwarted is 'passionate energy', 'afflicting passion'. So we suffer, but not from the object; what makes my suffering is my will being thwarted, which is only another way of saying 'not having what I want'.

Life frequently presents us with such suffering and as I struggle on, it appears that following the Buddha's Way is difficult because it often crosses my way. Then before long, speculating ahead about end-states as I am prone to do, the apprehension arises, 'If I am not allowed anything, if all goes bland without any feeling at all, will I then not lose the warm human touch, that which makes me human?' This contributes to the fear of losing myself, losing control, which inevitably arises at some stage or other on the Spiritual Path. At the bottom of it all is the panicky fear of 'what will then become of ME!'

To be free from the afflicting passions, however, equals deliverance from the straitjacket of 'I'; then there is no more clinging, and also no more coveting. But how is it then possible for a living being not to have any preferences? Coveting or not, passion or not, all need food, and food that nourishes them according to their kind – surely that is common to all? And as for us human beings, if we eat food gone bad we end up in hospital.

There is an answer to these my fears that is both helpful and accurate, and thus worthy of consideration. One not free from coveting, one craving fine food and then guzzling it, will 'experience the taste as well as the passion due to that taste'. The taste of the food will then be alloyed with the greed for it and so leads away from the pure taste and gets mixed up with such 'I'-centred judgements as 'more; should be a bit sweeter ... , hotter, overcooked again ... , oh scrumptious ... , more, more, I want more of this!' Experience in community life also teaches that a surprising number of young people and older ones, too, no longer know the taste of food and only judge it by their opinions, which come from their coveting and/or notions. They often recognize food by its looks rather than its taste! Is that why today we have so many passionate food fads? It is the nature of passions to carry us away.

The one who is free from passion just experiences the taste of the food he eats – he may enjoy it without making a pig of himself or may not much like it but eats enough to still his hunger and does so without being upset. Above all he will taste what he eats because he is not carried away by passion due to that taste.

This does, of course, not only apply to food and its taste but to all our senses. Hence seeing clearly is indeed the summum bonum of awakening from the delusions of the passions.

Here we need to become clear about the difference between the natural preferences that pertain to an individual form/body, and the passion which clings/covets and results from 'I want'. Much confusion and dissension has resulted from not having made this difference clear, even though there is an unmistakable gauge readily available. Every individual form is in itself unique as well as universal. The ginger cat that tries to fish the goldfish out of the pond, slim, with golden eyes, is unmistakably 'Leo' from next door, as well as unmistakably a cat, a mammal, a living being, something rather than nothing! Other cats which also come into the garden do not sit by the little pond for hours trying for some goldfish but all cats have the knack of invariably finding the coolest spot in summer and the warmest in winter. And although we are all human beings, no two of us walk exactly the same way, or brush our teeth the same way. We may prefer tea to coffee or vice versa, and need not labour ourselves to find convincing reasons why we do so – there are none; we just prefer the one or the other.

'Free from passion' then is, when offered a choice, to take the tea which I prefer and to enjoy it; and should there be none, then to drink the cup of coffee without further ado. This, however, changes drastically if I have fancied a cup of tea, and coffee is forthcoming instead! How frustrating and annoying – this is tea time! And to be given coffee when it is well known that I prefer tea! And just now, when I need to calm myself after a harrowing day – this is the last straw. Having looked forward to that cup of tea and now being denied it! Up rise the passions due to taste – not the taste of the food, but 'My Want', And just this is the difference. When 'I must have' flares, we are in thrall to the passions. Then we feel hot and bothered and try to manoeuvre, jockeying to get our way.

What this lengthy discussion tries to elucidate is that

the question about passion or no passion is not about life becoming bland but about the fear of 'I' not getting my way, of not being affirmed, of being diminished – and what then? The reassuring answer is, 'Don't worry'. Being weaned from my attachments makes for enjoyment of what is there rather than the coveting of some unavailable object which inhibits the enjoyment of what is present, is given.

It is common experience that obtaining what was hotly pursued does not answer, for after the triumphal 'at last', it soon pales. Moreover, if you allow me to have my will all the time, I'll soon begin to despise you or get bored and will walk out on you – although I have threatened that I will walk out on you if you will not let me have my own way! So, not having what I want is unsatisfactory, frustrating, lamentable – and having it does not answer either. The opposite then is to be realistic and, rather than I wanting things, circumstances, people and the world to be 'my way', to accept that I am not alone in this world, nor am I God Almighty. The world is as it is, with day and night, cold and warm. Although we cannot deny that our world suffers from a thousand ills, most of them we have brought about ourselves. So a modicum of restraint and humility would be in place. Rather than continue to rapaciously grab and demand, to cut back just a little bit. Then, if all of us live a bit more modestly and unpresumingly, not only would our world become a better place of itself, but we might gratefully rediscover the enjoyment of what is given and no longer chase after 'still more, higher, better'. Thus we would benefit ourselves as well as all of us; harmoniously together in spaceship earth, and be re-united with what we are – rather than a rampaging cancer battening on what is.

14 *Seeing but not being Deceived by Form*

A woman had married into a family of rank. Beautiful but vain, she had quarrelled with her husband and, decked and ornamented until she looked like a goddess, had left her home early in the morning to return to her family. On her way all men stared at her in admiration – except the Elder Mahatissa who sat by the roadside and took no notice of her. Piqued at seeing the venerable monk so unperturbed, the perversity of her nature caused her to laugh out loudly. The Elder looked up inquiringly and perceiving her teeth, suddenly saw her as only a bag of bones and at that fully awakened to enlightenment.

Meanwhile, the husband had discovered her flight and came in hot pursuit of his beautiful wife. He also saw the Elder, and asked him, 'Venerable One, have you seen a most beautiful woman come this way? Please, please, tell!' But the Elder did not even know whether he had seen a man or woman, and could only say that a bag of bones had been travelling along the road!

We have already met a similar theme in the question whether a life free from passion is not bland (No. 13, pp.69–74). The analogy made there pertains to food, but applies to all our doings. 'Picking and choosing' estranges us from being with what is, and so we miss out on life, which is one of the roots of our general feeling of dissatisfaction.

Naively, we also always assume that everybody in their right senses must think and feel as I do, and if you do not, apart from being wrong, you are also against me, and so aggression arises, or resentment.

Does it ever occur to us that we perceive according to our own views? This also means – our views being us – that we perceive according to how we are. Having read the same story or seen the same film, we tell different versions depending on what we 'took in' and what 'passed us by'. The critic only feeds us with his opinions of what we should like or find interesting. If we lack interest we may accept his views as our own, or we may refute his opinion and make up our own, equally biased mind.

The Elder in our story is then one who without passion and so without bias, sees the essentials of what actually is there – a bag full of bones!

But there is still more to our story. The Elder's pure perception does not only jolt the infatuated husband, we all may learn from it. The woman is quite obviously a vain hussy, and having possessed herself of all she could grab to deck herself out, off she went to the gay life, unencumbered by a husband to look after and care for – servant and slave to her own image and nothing else! And she was piqued by the ascetic on the roadside who seemed quite unimpressed by her swanking beauty bedecked with all possible finery, especially since she deemed herself not unlike a heavenly being! How the men stared at her as she waggled by, full of herself; and this old decrepit beggar did not even look at her, blind idiot three quarters in the grave already! Derisively she laughed out loud, partly to draw his attention and partly to drown the momentary uneasiness of not being noticed and thus no longer being affirmed as something, and something very special at that!

It was the laughter, the perception of sound, that drew the ascetic's attention and made him look up. The spiritual path does not demand a blanking out of the senses but their purification, emptying them of our views and opinions so that they can perceive truly, without distortion. The clarity of perceiving, hearing sound (of her laughter) and seeing the dazzling white (of her teeth), struck home and instantly bestowed enlightenment on the ascetic. As a result he is now mediator and ferryman to the other shore, he is at hand to help open the eyes of the husband who is in headlong pursuit of his lost love and property. 'Only a bag of bones!' It must have struck the husband with awe. To us, too, pondering the incident offers the chance of a true change of heart – from pursuit of what is perishable and changing to what holds true in all circumstances and gives succour and support. And even the woman – although we are not told – had her opportunity; although she refused it with a defiant laugh, who can say a seed had not fallen in and would sprout some time or other.

So here we have a meaningful coincidence, so seemingly arranged or preordained that, for us Westerners, it is hard to believe it could happen of its own accord, could actually be the general mode of things – a constant opportunity as the ever-present guide. This is likened to a pointing finger, always within the living web that nudges the right course of action, a small inner voice by which the inherent 'in-formation' that is the birthright of every form makes itself heard if we but listen quietly. Nor does it matter what we call it as long as we are aware of it and heed it. The gauge of being at one with the Dharma is heeding its nudging and its opportunities, which are constantly held out to each one of us. If misunderstood and taken personally, 'I' becomes inflated, arrogant and proud and so goes astray, whereas properly understood it is the greatest blessing, for it makes for the bliss of humbly being carried along by a cloud of grace.

15 *The Parable of the Raft*

Just as a man who has started on a long journey sees before him a great stretch of water, on this side full of doubts and fears, on the further side safe and free from fears; but there is no boat to cross over, no causeway for passing across from this to the other shore. So he sets about to collect grass, sticks, branches and leaves and binds them into a raft and, paddling, arrives safely on the yonder shore. There he thinks, 'This raft has been of great use to me – paddling on it across the water I have arrived on this shore. Should I now take it up on my head or my shoulders and carry it with me?'

But surely, that man has finished with the raft. Once crossed over and arrived at the further shore, he should think thus, 'This raft has been of great use, so hauling it up on the shore it could be left there while I continue on the Way.'

How does this parable then tally with the one about letting oneself plummet down the cliff (No. 23, pp.109–11)? Here we are advised to bestir ourselves diligently and resourcefully to reach the desired goal. Is this not a flagrant contradiction? 'God helps the sailor – but steer he must himself.'

Perhaps the first thing to realize is that there just is not, nor ever can be, a simple solution – much less one that fits all cases and contingencies. We ourselves are a contradiction, both wanting to have our own way and wanting to be told what to do. Or are we? For example, these days the training in our Zen Centre is established and settled in, our ways of training known. But to begin with, more often than not, somebody would come with the silliest but well-reasoned requests – 'Can I hold my hand just a little bit more like ... , etc., etc. Now, trainees may sit on a chair or on a cushion to meditate, and in case of physical problems, further adjustments are, of course, made, but wanting other exceptions is to 'have something special' to counteract the sense of shrinking. Although they themselves know that what they ask is not on, they still come and ask politely and conscientiously. The murderous look when denied shows clearly there is much more to the request than meets the eye. What's going on?

Of course we often want to do something we very well know we should not; if we endure that wanting (never repress it) and hatch it out, it will be productive of subsequent insight; but if we do it nevertheless, one of the consequences is a bad conscience. And now it becomes obvious why we asked – we want to do what we want but if we know we should not, we want permission so that we can do it with good conscience.

There is of course also the other, the hapless egotist, who is the shuttlecock of his own emotions. He is in need of a gentle but inexorable discipline that gives him the strength not to be carried away by each and every emotional eruption.

And so to the raft. For crossing the river of life, a vessel is necessary by means of which the 'other shore' may be reached. To build the raft demands skill and dedication – any old how will not do; for if it floated at all, the raft would fall apart in midstream. But even a trustworthy raft of its own accord floats downstream, not across; so a further skill has to be acquired, paddling across the stream without the raft

LOOK AND SEE

being upset. The river of life has many hazards, shoals, whirl-pools, stretches of racing currents – all dangerous to a flimsy raft. 'God helps the sailor but steer he must himself.'

And yes, sometimes the odds are too great, and in spite of all caution, the sailor is doomed – or is he? He struggles with all his might right to the end, for God helps the sailor if he does not give up. But if nothing avails and the portal opens, the sailor gives in, goes with it – to where he always has been.

So after all, the letting go and the paddling across are the two sides of a coin.

But here our sailor has paddled across and has arrived at the other shore. Our parable has come to an end, for only the question about the raft is raised. The sailor who arrived on the yonder shore is no longer the one who set out from this side. 'I' wanted to get rid of all I do not like, get beyond all pain and grievance and suffering. So I bestirred myself and learnt to build that raft and changed in the process. Patient endurance develops strength for sustained application; the many initial failures teach circumspection and humility. Thus a more experienced 'I' sets out, trusting myself to God who will help me if I skilfully bestir myself and steer rightly – his way, not mine! And so, after the hazards of the crossing, the one who arrives on the yonder shore is no longer the 'I' who set out, is a No-I who has handed himself over to God – has awakened to the Buddha-nature inherent in all beings. 'I' can have no conceptions of that other shore nor of arriving there. 'In the trackless the path comes to an end.'

My fond imagination that I can leave behind what I dislike and thus unburdened can now swan off into a new landscape, enjoying myself hugely – what a childish idea! Life, the Great

Life, is not like that; were it, it would long have become as polluted as we have polluted our rivers and oceans, our world here. Rather, what has dropped off is this naive, childish 'I' and only the question of the raft remains, the Great Use or Function of it but not on the yonder side. Beware now! The one who thinks to give it a contemptuous kick is still here, on this side; too impatient to labour on fashioning a safe raft, he gives himself airs and kicks his own failure. Such deceptions are of themselves short-lived.

If the river is really crossed, the other shore holds nothing, not even the raft; so what has crossed over has itself become a raft and will now help others build theirs and ferry them across. Yet although 'God helps the sailor, steer he must himself.' 'I liken my teaching to a raft', said the Buddha.

Perhaps if we, each of us, would endeavour to build our own raft from these teachings – not huge liners and cruise ships or oil tankers, but just from what is there at hand – sticks, branches, grass, perhaps a bit of driftwood – and diligently apply ourselves to that, we would have little time and inclination for the ever 'more, bigger, greater, better', the voracious appetites of 'I'. We would then realize that this insatiable compulsion is my misunderstanding of the longing for the other shore which, inborn, is beckoning today as of old, and always will. It is the longing of our own heart, which is the human heart, which is the universal heart, the heart of things, to become aware of itself. Which also re-states the importance of the human state with its reflective consciousness that makes such awareness possible.

CHAPTER II

From the Northern Training Scriptures

16 *The Two Ships*

The first Tang emperor stood on the bank of the Yangtse river and looked with pardonable pride at the throng of ships that plied up and down its mighty sweep. It was he, the emperor, who, caring for his people, had brought prosperity nation-wide. By his side stood his friend and spiritual guide, a great Zen master. 'See', said the emperor, 'the busy traffic on the river. Truly, the empire is flourishing.' 'But I see only two ships on the river', the Zen master replied. 'What are you talking about', the emperor wanted to know, 'when you can hardly see the water for all the shipping?' 'Two ships only', replied the Zen master firmly, 'the ship of gain, and the ship of fame.'

The emperor thought for a while, and then nodded. He undertook sweeping reforms, and set in train the cultural achievement to which the glorious Tang era attained.

The ship of gain and the ship of fame – more and more glorious achievement – and the golden age, or the new age, always just round the corner, already almost attained! At which time the next catastrophe shatters the fond illusion. And it all starts again, and again – and again. Nobody can deny that much that is good, great and helpful has emerged; medicine and science help to make life easier and longer. As our species has progressed, from the African Rift Valley to Neanderthal caves, to Swiss and other lakes settlements, French temple-caves, Mesopotamian villages and city-states, Babylonia and Egypt, Greece and Rome, through the Dark Ages, Chivalry, Renaissance, Reformation, to our Age of Enlightenment which, burgeoning, now threatens to black out the earth we live on – it is an oft-repeated tragic procession. Those two ships have dazzled us from the beginning. Why, oh why can we never be content – what compels us to chase those two ships, restlessly and ever faster? And sell our birthright in the process?

Could it be that somehow deep down and unbeknown to us, there is a half-perceived longing, a primordial hope as old as our fall and expulsion from Paradise, that with the spoils of those ships we might buy our way back – past that angel with the flaming sword who guards it against our fallen state? There is no way 'back into' Paradise but, so we have been assured, there is a way 'forward into' it. However, this way exacts the severing of our attachment to those two fatal ships. 'Unless you become as little children'. Not childish – a childish adult is a sore spectacle. Not spoilt brats either. 'As little children', not yet aware of the irresistible attraction of the two ships and so content as long as hunger is stilled and no pain is felt; the child at play – it busily discovers a whole world.

We have so much today that makes our lives easier; but what do we do with our 'free' time? It oppresses us and so we fritter it away, actually try 'to kill time'. How poor we have become, how we have squandered our cultural and spiritual values! Instead of entering our rich inheritance and making it our own and adding our contribution to it, we deny it because we cannot be bothered to grow into it. So we belittle what is great, pull it down to our ill-mannered level. Not only the football hooligans, the media, too, encourage the trend. Bread and circuses were offered as sops to the Romans and then the once mighty empire crashed down; the comparison with football and telly is uncomfortably close. And the two ships? War or not war, forward and back – another burgeoning and another destruction. And we continue to seek 'the criminal' to brand him!

But God, who fashioned us in his likeness, knows his creatures and, taking it out of our bloodstained hands, reserves revenge as his prerogative. Could we but heed him and abstain from looking outside to find a scapegoat, we might find the criminal in our own heart. There, by the mercy that God shows to the repenting sinner and out of the Compassion that the Buddha has for all beings, we might acknowledge this dark brother and labour patiently to make him able to partake in our human, cultural riches so that he no longer needs to chase the two ships; and as we then settle down together to play the great game of Life, we discover how little is necessary to be happy and content. Just this is what we can share with our neighbours.

To sing because the heart is full, to praise the glory of what is, which, not being ours, is not to be possessed or despoiled. To be recharged again and again by the beauty in the great and the small, as it is, to feel gratitude for all that is given and have no demands, rather to give and do oneself as required for the wellbeing of all, to always find time to stand and see and be moved, and to express it in deed and word and thought, in song and chant and praise – new variations of the same old divine melody – that is how time is gracefully spent, and time there now is since the two ships have sailed away over the horizon and have been lost sight of. Instead of chasing those phantom ships, the heart sings as it partakes in the glory of the Divine, for 'the Earth is the Lord's, and the fullness thereof.'

17 *The Lost Son*

The only son of a rich merchant had left home and gone astray. In spite of his efforts he fell on evil days and was reduced to beggary. Eventually he joined a group of vagrants.

The merchant meanwhile had desperately searched for his son but all his efforts were futile and in grief and sorrow he decided to sell off his estates and move to another region. There he set up business again, and again this flourished and soon he was once more the rich merchant-prince with a palatial mansion.

One day a couple of ragged beggars rather timidly entered the forecourt; the merchant happened to see them and recognized his own son in one of them. Overjoyed, he was just about to rush out and embrace him when the young man's being ill-at-ease became obvious and the merchant realized that any hasty approach would only scare the beggars away.

He sent his overseer to speak to them but they took fright and ran away. The merchant quickly instructed his personal servant to don beggar's clothes and follow them. He was to tell them that the rich house was always friendly to those in need and offered work to all who wished for it. Thus the young man was enticed to come back. He was allotted a menial task and a corner in the stable yard to sleep. Only slowly, at cautious intervals, was the young man then given more responsible jobs to do. He showed himself both willing and capable, and so his father, still not daring to reveal himself, slowly brought him up so as to be capable of taking over the business.

Years had passed when finally the ageing merchant decided that the time was ripe. He had all his staff and business associates gathered and with tears of joy revealed that the young man who had worked his way up in the business and was now capable of running it, was his own dear son and heir, and had him installed as such.

From of old, parables have been a favourite vehicle to express universal truths. All religions have made use of them and thus they have become embedded in the cultural inheritance of the people who profess them. Many of the themes recur regularly, are universal but inflected in ways specific to a given people to whom they become part of the cultural continuum even if the religious connotations are all but lost.

Thus, irrespective of its Christian content, we have all been brought up on the parable of the Prodigal Son – the great joy of being reunited again with what was lost. We find the same theme in a scripture of the Northern School of Buddhism, the Lotus Sutra, but there the stress is somewhat different.

The young man comes begging to the father's mansion without knowing it. Shaken by its splendour, he hesitates to enter the yard, afraid of being chased away, perhaps even being punished. But the father has recognized his long-lost son in him. Seeing the beggar's fear and his turning away, he sends a servant to offer him work, just sweeping the yard.

Only gradually he advances him, has him educated and finally offers partnership. Now the announcement of the relationship can be made safely and the young man takes his place in his father's mansion.

It should need no comment – yet there is nowadays an abounding conviction that a learning period or apprenticeship is not really necessary and that I can do it if I but put my mind to it, or, if I feel that I want to. Nothing gives me pause and 'like a bull in a china shop' I 'wade in where angels fear to tread'. Yet I am also surprisingly prone to all kinds of isms and attacks of irrational fears. Perhaps the story of the Lost Son could be a pointer?

Swashbuckling hooliganism, sharp-dealing one-upmanship, or short-sighted sentimentality with its concomitant lurking aggression are no substitute for the solidity and dignity of a well-rounded individual who is no longer swayed by the winds of passion or by fashionable trends. Thus we do well to heed the message: the young man's gentling progress of nurturing and cultivation, a labour of love to fulfil an inherent potential on the one hand, and on the other the cautious, caring, responsible and informed approach of the father, who can contain himself even though circumstances seem to impel him twice to some rash action that would have been counterproductive and bound to end up in sorrow and lamentation.

Our language still has echoes of such experiences: The cultivated 'gentle-man', made rather than born, who can no longer be carried away by any emotional ups or downs and has become a dependable and caring member of the community.

18 *The Tree-Pruning Master*

A Master Pruner, famous for his skill with even the highest trees, had an apprentice due to undergo examination for his master degree. A high and dangerous tree was selected for the purpose and many people assembled to watch. Up climbed the apprentice to the very top, started pruning, and slowly worked his way down through the branches. Motionless under the tree stood the master himself, following his every move. Just as the apprentice was lowering himself down to the last branches, only a few yards above ground, the master yelled, 'Care! Take care!'

The apprentice completed his task successfully. One of the bystanders, puzzled, asked the master, 'When the young man was aloft swaying on that high top, you kept silent. Why did you call out when he was almost down to the ground and out of danger. Even if he had then slipped, he would not have hurt himself much!' 'But that's just it', replied the Master Pruner, 'Up there, he knows himself how dangerous it is and takes good care. But after hours of hard and dangerous work, when nearly down to the ground – that is when caution slips and accidents occur'.

'Pride comes before the fall.' It applies here, too – but in a rather unexpected way. Our daily life is full of little slips, avoidable with a bit of care and caution. The story tells us how.

Paying attention to what is being done, being one with the doing, with the situation, heedfully, carefully, circumspectly, collectedly getting on with the doing – in this collected oneness the mind does not wander, no disconnected thoughts intrude, no daydreams, no speculations, not even a self-conscious awareness of 'I' doing 'it'. Up in the top branches, danger exacts such collection, and skill shows the way. But such concentrated application together with the physical exertion is quite tiring and as yet the young man lacks experience. Self-consciousness comes back, 'Ah, well done', or, 'Now safe', or 'Test passed' and in this momentary 'dis-connection' from what is, the slip occurs – on the tree, in the workshop, in the kitchen, on the ladder or what have you.

'Familiarity breeds contempt', and becoming careless because of that familiarity is productive of mishaps if not worse. It is the little things that trip us up again and again, our own heedlessness and silliness.

From our side, we need to acquaint ourselves with the nature of things so that we can co-operate rather than go against or unwittingly offend. The one who approaches a nervous young horse silently from behind asks to be kicked; or if I put down the fish on the kitchen table with Pussy on the chair next to it, and go to ring you up with the latest news, it is no good blaming Pussy for the fish gone and scales all over the kitchen – it is the nature of a cat to love fish; I as much as gave it to her, didn't I?

This, taken to heart and acted upon will result in less accidents and less blaming others or the 'outside' for the consequences of our own heedlessness. How much more peace of mind and equanimity such an attitude creates! And it may set an example to others, younger, not so experienced. Like an old mountaineer who will neither hurry nor tarry, he just keeps on walking, heedfully. Or climbing. And he comes safely back again.

19 *The Spider*

A monk of long standing and diligent found that latterly when he sat himself down to meditate, a spider appeared in his vision. He tried to ignore it, but each time the spider seemed to grow and finally became huge and threatening. At his wit's end, he went to consult the master who suggested he kept on with his meditation with all his might. But to no avail – on the contrary, the spider's belly began to swell and looked venomous, and the monk was now afraid for his life. Again he asked the master's advice. 'Well, if it comes to it,' said the master, 'what are you thinking of doing?'

'I have been pondering', said the monk, 'but the spider came without being asked; by sheer ill will it is out for my life. I know that as a Buddhist monk I must not take life, and I would not willingly do so. But here I am, some thirty years in service to the Buddha, a mature and disciplined monk and if I may mention it, not without attainment! And now this spider! Well, if it comes to the point – and it seems that it has – there is no other way open for me but to kill it.'

'Just once more go and meditate', said the master, giving him a bit of chalk, 'and if the spider really reaches out for you, do not kill it but make a cross on its belly quickly and then run and come to me.' Of course the monk obeyed the master's suggestion but hardly had he sat himself down when the spider, now only a venomous belly, appeared and seemed to overcome him. Trembling with terror and loathing, he just managed to chalk the cross on the swollen belly and run to the master where he stammered out that he could no longer endure it and would have to stick a knife into that poisonous monster. The master ordered him to lift up his robe – and there, on his own belly, was the chalk mark he had drawn!

This seems to be a weird story of long ago – the heated imagination of a secluded monk. Come to think of it, rather like the desert fathers of yore who also physically fought with the devil – and had their scratch marks to prove the encounter. Does such a story have any relevance in our ordinary daily lives? Quite apart from our phobias – spiders and creepy-crawlies in general are fond targets – do we not have problems that beset us, wants or ambitions that ride us, somebody in our working or family environment the mere thought of whom 'drives us mad'?

Well, to the desert fathers the devil was every bit as real as our problems are to us – and so was that spider to that monk.

As a youngster in the early 1930s, I was desperately keen to learn to ride a bicycle. But I was also secretly afraid of bicycles because of an early memory of being taken for a ride on a bicycle which ended with a bad spill and sharp grit lacerating hands and knees. Nevertheless, I applied myself and could already wobble along, but was very clumsy in dismounting. Hitting a large stone would invariably unsaddle me. There were plenty about and whenever one was looming in the distance, I did my utmost to avoid it but it was a direct hit every time! Some forty years later, I formulated this as: 'Whatever we fear or hate, that we give power over ourselves', that is, the concentrated attention we accord it truly 'concretizes' it!

Since fear is but the other side of 'I', I cannot control it – at best only evade it. Buddhism points out an effective remedy for this in the parable of the Anger-Eating Demon (No. 9, pp.51–54) and from it we may gain a deeper understanding of the profound insight/warning that our story conveys.

So when our neighbour or colleague with whom we have quarrelled or whom we envy, takes on the mask of a devil and has the power to wake us up in the small hours of the night, we do well to look inside ourselves. And there we actually find a force which is 'my own' reaction to that person, thing or circumstance; it is that which holds me in thrall, not the outside. Moreover, my quick and hasty assumptions are then made up of my wants, refusals, exclusions and fears which act like a lens. Focussed and projected they produce 'heat', the afflicting passions which are also notoriously blind. These are the cause of unskilful behaviour, aggression, etc. If strong enough, they may even 'concretize' into psychosomatic afflictions which are subjectively real enough or also as misperceptions, perverting the senses, and which in extreme cases can cause something like poltergeist phenomena.

I, the reasonable, ordinary I that I believe myself to be in cold blood, scoff at such ideas – what nonsense! That is until I am reminded of, or confronted by, my 'bête noire' at which point I am suddenly transformed into a trembling or raging bundle of conflicting emotions. And yes, it happens to us all – the newspapers live on it!

To this also belong the tensions of modern life, caused by our naive assumptions of 'ever more, ever better'. In sport last year's record is to be broken this year. In job and office ever more is expected; we are lured on by advancement and perks, or threatened by dismissal, and so take on ever more tasks – until it slops over either into fraud or nervous breakdowns. Again, the newspapers keep us informed. Added to this is the relentless pressure of society and the media to do, speak and think this or that.

But how to counteract or at least to withstand all that influence as well as the quite ruthless drives that possess us? These latter are not just 'outside' and no scapegoat needs to be found – whether threat or lure, it is my reaction to them which counts, and accordingly my response will be either dictated by this emotional reaction or will be based on a 'clear seeing' in which self-deception no longer prevails. In the grip of self-deception, fired by the emotional energy, I believe myself to be completely objective and impartial; this, however, can easily be disproved. But worse, a ruthlessness which can only be termed 'a-human' clings underneath to that tremendous energy of the 'fired' state. It is from that state that our so-called 'inhuman' deeds arise and from which we perpetrate our heedless, impassioned, blind actions which we may even deem to be well-intentioned and 'good'.

We are helpless in the grip of these powers, for individually, alone, we do not have the strength to withstand them – their force is 'numinous' and geared to overpower 'I'. In times when our cultural and religious values were still intact, these powers in their sublime and demonic mode were conceived respectively as God and devil. But actually, all times and societies have accorded the mantle of divinity to them and as such they had set limits and tabooed excesses. 'The Almighty takes good care that trees do not grow high enough to pierce heaven', says an Austrian proverb.

Whether at tribal level or in high cultures, religious and social mores are means to at least hold those forces in check and at best to transform them and with them the individual 'carrier'. Over and above the social adaptation thus secured, the common aim of all religions is the actual transformation of the individual.

And in the absence of such values? Once again, the newspapers tell the grim story. But different from the newspapers, training stories and parables carefully set out the causes and advocate ways to undo them. The surprising, fascinating, heart-warming and heartening fact is that, looked at carefully, they are all perceived to 'speak the same language'. We only have to learn to interpret the expressions rather than to cling to the word-level only. Thus, the Christian 'Into Thy hands, Oh Lord, I commend my spirit' and the Buddhist 'There is no such thing as an independent I' state one and the same fact. This fact is well known in everyday usage as 'good' or as selflessness. It still has an emotional appeal, although we rarely bother ourselves to grapple with its true meaning.

The way of transformation is the religious way, the way not back but forward towards 'the end of suffering' (Buddhist), the 'New Jerusalem' (Christian). It leads towards wholeness, at-one-ment with 'the way all things really are'. The heart of itself inclines towards this way as 'its own' but in the absence of a valid framework for it, the heart grows wild and hungry, is swerved by any fancy that is in the air, and heedlessly charges around without let or hindrance.

So, the cure would then seem to be an insight in the radiance of which 'I' fades away. In the shift or transformation consequent to such an 'in-sight', the individual awakens to his True Nature that was inherent anyway, only covered up by the clouds of my likes and loathings. With that, the bonds fall off that held the individual captive in a narrow 'I'-biased view with assumptions derived from blind passions, forced by them into heedless, unskilful actions. Now liberated, the individual realizes his/her humanity and has irrevocably become a human being, capable of remaining one and acting as such under all circumstances, good, bad or indifferent. That is the nature of a gentle-man or gentle-woman and includes the cultivation of cultural values as well as the gentling of crude energy. In that it also generates a degree of fearlessness which manifests as a general but well-informed goodwill which is very different from the heedless emotionality and underlying aggression that drives both the do-gooder and the saboteur.

Over and above, yet based on and grounded in this state of our true humanity is then the inner, or spiritual Way as such, which by careful training along well-mapped stages helps the devotee to divest himself even further and pull off remnants of 'I'-induced habit patterns of actions as well as of thinking. Along such a course we inevitably become acquainted with each and all the inadequacies and dark spots of our individual make-up. Such a demanding practice can only be undertaken validly by virtue of the human state and its accrued energy/strength/power. Which points us to a re-reading of the term 'virtue' and all it implies: obedience, discipline, sacrifice, observances – not as a 'must' but 'for the love of' and hence 'in service', a labour of love, joyful and rewarding even if hard in places, and open-hearted, that is not denying or refusing anything, but rather making good use of what is given here and now.

Thus, the senses themselves become gateways of this harmonious flow of actions.

A wrestler was immensely strong and highly skilled. In private he defeated even his teacher, but in public the youngest pupil could throw him. In his trouble he went to see the Zen master at a nearby temple by the sea, and asked for counsel. 'Stay in this temple tonight', said the master, 'and listen to the waves of the sea. Feel yourself to be the waves. Forget you are a wrestler and become those huge waves sweeping all before them.' Then the teacher left him alone in the Shrine Room.

The wrestler tried to think only of the waves, but he thought of many things. Then gradually he began to hear the waves. They rolled larger and larger as the night wore on. They swept away the flowers in the vases before the Buddha. They swept away the vases. Even the bronze Buddha was swept away. By dawn the temple was only surging water, and the wrestler sat there with a faint smile on his face.

That day he entered a public competition, and won every bout. From then on, no one in Japan could ever throw him, and he became known as 'Great Wave'.

I am a bungler; every 'I' is – either overdoing or under-doing things. Either I so much want to do them right, to show how good I am – and fluff it every time, my performance positively creaking with 'I'-intention or pride. Or else I am so embarrassed in public that I can't do a thing right. I feel all eyes are on me and am practically lamed by my self-consciousness. I long to be free, spontaneous; so I try to act and it is a clanger! The more I care, the more I try, the worse it gets; yet alone I seem to have little trouble. A great Japanese

Zen master succinctly sums up this universal attitude as 'At home, a tiger; in public, a scared pussycat.' And there is, of course, the swashbuckler, too, and the charmer and conman. This story is concerned with excessive self-consciousness.

Our wrestler was such a man; he had great skill, but had not yet found his own middle, his inner centre of gravity, his True Face. His technique was excellent, and he was already entrusted to teach. Indeed, within the closed walls of the training hall he could even defeat his teacher, but any kind of public show saw him at the mercy of his youngest pupil. Whatsoever he did and tried, he could not overcome his impediment. Then he heard of a Zen master nearby and decided to go there and ask for help.

It so happened that his temple was close by the sea-shore. The Master listened to the wrestler's tale and nodded; however specific and singular a problem seems to 'me', at root it is a very general one.

Here we may reflect once more on the recurring theme of 'I and my problems'. As this story exemplifies, 'I and my problem' are one. I feel myself separate as a unique individual – and the Zen master knows that there is no separation and that all different forms, by their very uniqueness, express what is 'grave and constant', the Dharma, the laws of Nature, or whatever name we have for it; names are pointers only.

So again, I being my own problem means that I am my own obstruction that hinders me from freely flowing with what is, for the benefit of all including myself. Whatever reasons I cite for this obstruction, whatever pictures I paint of it which I then project outward and, thus 'concretized', I now take these ghosts for real – it is all at root one and the same for us human beings with our 'I'-bias and hence mistaken identity. The Fourth Patriarch already exhorted us, 'Stick to the root, do not bother about the branches'. Do not go on chasing branches, chasing pictures that seemingly arise of themselves as my reasons for answers sought and impelled by my likings and loathings. We are reminded of the Parable of the Poisoned Arrow (No. 2, pp.25–29). How these stories reflect and highlight each other, stressing different aspects yet always pointing us back to the root! Similarly spiritual practices and teachers guide us upon that Way. They have nothing to teach, they just point and point and again point out the Way which we ourselves must walk.

So our wrestler explained his problem to the master who, aware of the universality of it, suggested a night in the temple contemplating the waves of the sea. In the deepening night the wrestler sat all alone and all kinds of thoughts rose unbidden, filled him, changed into others, wave after wave of thoughts rolling in and subsiding, in an endless round.

Late into the night, in his inner surging, the wrestler suddenly became aware of the sea, its waves also surging, rolling in, sweeping in ever larger and more thunderous, beginning to engulf flowers, vases, even the Buddha himself – all that was there; and in the end nothing was there, no wrestler either; all was only surging water. A faint smile swept over the face of the wrestler, perhaps like the smile that was on Mahakasyapa's face when he saw the Buddha silently raising the flower – at which, so tradition says, the Buddha acknowledged Mahakasyapa as his heir and successor.

Our wrestler, too, 'went back home', for there is the 'way up' to that height of wave or mountain or whatever which engulfs, sweeps away and noughts 'I'. At which the realization 'rises' or perhaps 'sinks in' of the truth of No-I which equals 'for the sake of all'. So the wrestler goes back, the 'way down,' and takes up 'his thing' again, which is wrestling, and from then on is invincible. And his name? O-Nami – The Great Wave.

21 *The Taming of the Harp*

Long ago in the Longmen Gorge stood a mighty tree, a veritable king of the forest. It reared its head to talk to the stars; its roots struck deep into the earth, mingling their bronzed coils with those of the silver dragon that slept beneath. One day a mighty wizard came and made of this tree a wondrous harp. But the stubborn spirit of the tree still clung to it and although a magnificent instrument, it would be tamed only by the greatest of musicians. The wizard presented the harp to the Imperial Court where for long the instrument was treasured but all efforts to draw melody from its strings were in vain. The greatest musicians of the day tried, yet there came from the harp but harsh notes of disdain, ill-according with their songs. The harp refused to recognize a master.

One day Bai Ya, prince of harpists, happened to come. Gently he caressed the harp as one might seek to soothe an unruly horse, and softly he touched the chords. He sang of nature and the seasons, of high mountains and flowing waters, and, lo, all the memories of the tree awoke! Once more the breath of spring played amidst its branches. The young cataracts, as they danced down the ravine, laughed to the budding flowers. Then were heard the dreamy voices of summer with its myriad insects, the gentle pattering of rain, the call of a cuckoo. Now a tiger's roar, and the valley echoing it. In the desert night of autumn, the frosted grass gleamed like swords in the moon. Now winter reigned, snowflakes swirled and rattling hailstones beat with fierce delight upon the frozen boughs.

Then Bai Ya changed the key and sang of love. The forest sighed like an enchanted lover lost in thought. On high, like a haughty maiden, a cloud swept by, and in its passing trailed long shadows on the ground, black like despair. Again the mood was changed; Bai Ya sang of war, of clashing steel and trampling steeds. In the harp arose the tempest of Longmen and the dragon rode the lightning as a thundering landslide crashed down the hills.

The celestial monarch was enthralled and asked Bai Ya the secret of his victory over the harp. 'Sire', he replied, 'others have failed because they sang but of themselves. I left the harp to choose its theme, and truly knew not whether the harp had been Bai Ya or Bai Ya was the harp.'

Although a commentary seems superfluous, yet we of a later age might well miss nuances without which the great lines of this story cannot be realized, brought to life. For that we need to make our own hearts into the harp.

This and the previous story, The Great Wave, are teaching parables from the 'Ways' and are more explicit in content than the Buddhist ones. The Longmen Gorge is both spectacular and dangerous and has held the imagination from of old. The river races through it in mighty rapids, dragons live at its bottom – a truly primeval landscape, wild, untamed, utterly itself and self-contained. On its cliff stands a gigantic tree, its roots so deep that they intertwine with the coils of the river dragon far, far below; its mighty branches reach upwards, soaring towards heaven.

This gigantic tree has won freedom from all ensnarements and stands fast in all weathers. Karmically speaking, its life as a tree is nearing its end; as a tree it 'has done what was to be done'. Now, mutely reaching towards heaven, with the wind whistling, roaring or sighing in its branches and playing the old melody of 'coming to be, ceasing to be' – does the tree know, does its heart or spirit long to express what it is full of? Now the tree spirit has outgrown its tree-nature, is no longer bound by it; it is due to 'go into change', into transformation. Not only does renewal work cyclically, repeating the same, but also as transformation of form and consciousness. Although all forms hum the song celestial, the fullness of its orchestration and expression depends on and grows with forms, with their development towards ever greater awareness. All transformation, development and evolution strive towards that awareness in which the universe may become conscious of itself. Self-consciousness in the form of 'I' is a short-circuited aberration of this, hence the Buddha's teaching that consciousness is universal, is the True Nature, True Face, Buddha-Nature; it is what we have always been, are, and wish for. This joyful awareness even amidst suffering is inborn in all forms and strives, consciously or unconsciously, towards its fulfilment.

And so our tree, towering above on its crag, is bound by a form that can no longer adequately express what fills its heart, what 'animates' it. It is due for transformation; its gigantic spirit has broken free already and has the magic gift of transmuting the tree into a wonderful harp, an instrument now capable of giving voice to that song celestial. But it still lacks a player, for the wind is no longer adequate and some of the ragged stubbornness of the tree still clings to the harp and the spirit that gave it form. So that spirit, too, is in need of transformation and hence the need for a musician greater than all others who can gentle and humanize the stubborn spirit and play this magnificent harp. Therefore this splendid instrument fittingly ends up as the treasure of the Imperial Court. There all the great musicians of the domain tried their hand at it, but the harp remained mute, or worse still, it only twanged a few harsh notes of disdain in response to their utmost striving to force the harp to sound.

That was until the day Bai Ya happened to come to court and heard about the harp.

Now Bai Ya was the acknowledged master harpist of his time, and it is said that his playing accurately rendered the surging of the sea, the sighing of the wind, the height of a rugged mountain, or lushness of a green valley, storm and sunshine, but also human sentiments, love and longing, anger and war. Yet although Bai Ya had the greatness and skill to faultlessly render the song celestial in human terms, the real song, once heard, is over and above what can be expressed even by the greatest of human potential. It is hinted at by expressions like 'heard with the eye', and completely fills a human heart that is empty and therefore receptive. 'Those who know do not speak' – they have become one with it and so, aware of it, they sound in human terms this soundless song celestial in whatever they happen to be, harpist or cobbler alike.

The great Bai Ya was aware of both his humanity with its limitations and that in his True Nature he was freely and at one with what is, that he himself was informed by this song and its tremendous power to which all responds. Gently he laid his hands on that stubborn harp that longed to be tamed but would yield to none but the greatest.

This is the search for true transformation, the bipolar readying for it, the long and often painful process from the rugged wildness of my way as I see it, to the gentle humanity which, having recognized what is more than I and yielded to it, has already the dignity and stance of an individual form or carrier of what is. With that also arises the longing towards a conscious awareness of this. As inspiration it also renders the power and zest out of which it is then naturally lived, expressed in the life and actions of an aware individual.

Hence the importance of the taming, gentling process that all spiritual traditions enjoin so that, softened up, the change from 'I only' to 'What Is' may take place. It is the meek who will inherit the kingdom. The form is not 'broken' but transmuted. What has to break is the stubborn rigidity, the egg-shell. The shell is not the egg; what is inside, the egg, properly hatched, is then transmuted into the chicken which emerges when the shell breaks and what is inside is ripe to burst the shell.

So in Bai Ya the giant tree spirit has now taken human form. All forms are manifestations of the Spirit, of that celestial song which actually has no form and no location. What was once the tree-devata and then became the wizard is now transformed into the great musician Bai Ya, who gently lays his hands on what was the rugged tree and is now the stubborn harp. It wants to yield and is ready to do so, but will only be awakened by the knowing, gentling touch of a master player; to that it now gives over, responds wholly, fully, totally, at last released from its old restraints. It sings of all it was – the moods and forms of nature, and of human nature. It and Bai Ya are one again, the tree and its devata, harp and spirit, instrument and master player, playing that melody to which all human hearts incline, and respond, and in which they recognize themselves and all that is. The harp attuned to the variations of the one theme, renders them perceptible, animated by the Spirit, by the mysterious, inexpressible, ineffable, intangible motivater that enlivens all forms and without which nothing is, for there is no such thing as dead matter.

How can such a melody be anything other than great, gripping and lifting the human heart in mighty aspiration? The huge tree of old that mutely raised its branches can now, transformed, give full expression to it. How different, how totally other is this great theme from the paltry droning of myself only.

22 *An Old Man of Eighty*

At the beginning of the illustrious Tang era, there lived in the capital an old gentleman renowned for the depth of his insight into the teachings of Master Kung (Confucius) and for his gentlemanly courtesy and integrity. He heard that somewhere in the deep, barbarian south a new teaching had arisen that was supposed to be even more profound than that of Confucius. The scholar found this rumour intolerable; and since there was no one else of such penetrating insight, in spite of his eighty years, he decided to undertake the hazardous and difficult journey himself to settle the issue. No trouble is too much in the pursuit of truth. Finally, after weeks of courageously endured discomfort, he arrived at the Zen monastery the master of which was said to have deep and genuine insight. The old gentleman introduced himself, said what had brought him there all the way from the capital and suggested that, should the other agree, they would each lay out their insight to the other and then – as two gentlemen – they would decide which of the two was the more profound.

Agreed, the Confucian started and in the course of some three hours laid bare the whole of Master Kung's teachings, with his own comments, and then politely asked his host to now please expound his insight. But the Zen Master only said, 'To avoid doing harm as much as possible, and to do good as much as possible – this is the teaching of all the Buddhas.'

The old gentleman was pardonably incensed, 'I have held nothing back, have honourably declared my purpose and laid bare all the profundity of the Confucian teachings. And you, you answer me with a little jingle which every three-year old child knows by heart! Are you mocking me?'

'By no means', replied the Zen Master, 'I rather honour you for undertaking such a long and difficult journey in search of truth. However, though it is true that every three-year old child knows this verse, yet, as you see yourself, even a man of eighty fails to live up to it!'

Truth is simple; what is complicated is not truth itself, but our ideas about truth. Truth only seems difficult because it is complicated by my bias, partiality, opinions, all of which need to be cleared out; this, in fact, amounts to being transformed into what basically they are – force, energy, power, but not 'mine'.

A Zen saying tersely states, 'Trees and water – not trees and water – trees and water.' Our story, popular in Zen Buddhism, elucidates this in the manner of a Chinese brush painting that sketches the outlines and leaves the beholder to flesh it out.

So we have the Confucian gentleman. Without going into detail, the making of a gentleman in ancient China was fundamentally by study, learning, and passing the state examinations – which were open to all. Such a gentleman was expected to uphold the Confucian virtues of benevolence, propriety, courtesy, knowledge and loyalty. For sustaining such conduct, the passions need to be curbed because, though not yet transformed, they are then at least no longer liable to break out into conflagration and carry us away. Actually, just this is also the mark of a gentleman in our Western culture-continuum – by his education a gentleman is made foolproof against the soaring of passions. He is thus cultured in the sense of being learned and appreciative of beauty, and on that basis is capable of valid judgements and sustained application without being swerved by personal bias or opinion. Courtesy, benevolence and loyalty or faithfulness are natural concomitants to it. Hence it is said that a gentleman recognizes a gentleman even if they come from quite different cultures.

Since this has to do with the transformation of the emotional energy, the same qualities are also cultivated in Zen training, though not for their own sake alone. As a contemporary Zen master expressed it: the (Confucian) gentleman and a man of Zen are not the same, but they have a lot in common.

Such a Confucian gentleman, old, well-settled, with much experience and deep insight into Master Kung's teachings hears a rumour that somewhere in the deep south, inhabited only by uncouth barbarians, there had sprung up a teaching more profound than any of the Confucian tenets. This was unbearable – how could there be! Such slanderous rumours had to be scotched! Yet to do so demanded from him, as a gentleman, not to go on hearsay alone but to find out himself. The dilemma was that he was old and frail yet nobody was his equal in depth of understanding. There was nothing for it but to go himself, however rigorous and dangerous such a journey might be. It would take months to accomplish it. And there was a very real possibility of perishing on the road due to his age and the dangers of such an adventure into barbary, with bandits and wild beasts to boot. But being a gentleman and thus honour bound, there was no other way than to set out and accomplish the journey himself. Finding his way to the region, he there heard of a recently established Buddhist school called Zen and of the renown of the master who headed a large new monastery.

Having arrived there at last, he asked for the master, introduced himself, stated the purpose of his visit and suggested that they should each propound their insight so that – and this is deeply significant – as gentlemen they could both decide whose teaching was the more profound. For the Confucian gentleman it was inconceivable that anyone supposedly having much understanding and hence great learning could be anything other than a gentleman. And he believed that as two gentlemen they could not have different judgements or opinions, or be swayed by personal predilection! What a lesson for us to ponder who tend to be swayed without even being aware of it! 'Trees and water – not trees and water.' But there are gradations.

The Zen master declared himself agreeable to the proposal, then politely asked the guest to start proceedings. The Confucian laid bare the deepest meaning and his understanding without subterfuge or holding anything back; and it took him some hours. The Zen master listened attentively all the while, without interruption. Finally the Confucian scholar, with a bow, had done and now invited his host to hold forth. The Zen master's reply, however, was short, just a quotation from the earliest and best known Buddhist scripture, the Dhammapada. In all Buddhist or Buddhist-influenced countries its verses are common knowledge.

Our gentleman, on hearing this, was pardonably incensed; he had braved discomfort and danger, had throughout acted according to the five great virtues of a gentleman, had held nothing back, and now to be treated like that! 'Even a three-year old child knows this jingle by heart! Even the barest rumour of your great insight would indicate that you were a gentleman, so how can you mock another gentleman?'

But the Zen Master quietly pointed out, 'Yes, it is true, every child knows the saying – but as you see, even a gentleman of eighty does not always live up to it.' However deep the insight, however great the cultivated virtues, if they cannot be lived under all, even the most provoking circumstances, there is still something lacking – and just that is what the

Zen school insists on. It emphasizes the full and complete transformation of all the afflicting passions into the Buddha-nature which is inherent in all sentient beings but is clouded over in us by the delusions of a separate selfhood with its concomitant attachments. Though commonly rendered as the 'cutting off' or 'extirpation' of these afflicting passions, which themselves are a diversification of the Fires, it is, in fact, not a 'cutting off' in the sense of getting rid of by repression but is the valid and lasting transformation of the emotional or psychic energy itself.

Thus, trees are again trees, and water is water. Starting and ending with trees as trees and water as water. Are the two stages the same, having parted and been reunited? When asked, a Zen priest said, 'In a way they are, but there is yet a fundamental difference – the infant sees trees as trees, etc. But then something frightens him or upsets him or he gets hurt and yells out 'Mummy!' No need for this yell in the third stage!'

To be free of fear – of all fear: panicky fear, fear of loss, fear of diminution, fear of pain, fear of death and fear of life – that is another way of looking at transformation, the aim of all spiritual ways, from 'I' to a whole, warm-hearted, true human being.

23 *The Thousand-foot Cliff*

A man has lost his footing on a thousand-foot cliff; as he begins to slither down, one hand happens to grab a stout root. There he now hangs holding on to the root with one hand, the other and his feet dangling over the yawning abyss. Can he let go?

This is a famous Zen question. It is included in this collection because it points out a perennial problem – and its solution.

A proverb states, 'A healthy man has a thousand wishes, the sick man has one only.' And so it is with all of us. Even if not clearly formulated, we all have a thousand wants, likes, preferences, etc. But occasionally, and not necessarily due to illness, all these seem to come together into one, and we feel that if only I could have this one – whatever 'this one' might be – I would be satisfied, not mind anything else; 'if only' I had my health again, or my lost love, or whatever I long for.

This is hanging on the thousand-foot cliff, clutching the stout root. If only! Life hangs us onto that cliff at least a few times, but we do not recognize it. Frantically struggling, we somehow manage to scramble back up again, and so here we are once more, complete with our thousand wishes. As a consequence we become ever more demanding and nothing, neither reason nor principles, bids a halt to our unbridled wants, rights or opinions. The result is increasing pollution, impoverished environment, and an overpopulation that ensures things will become worse, for it is obvious that the more of us there are, the less the individual gets or counts.

So what should be done? Life hangs us onto that thousand-foot cliff; and yet amazingly, the more spoilt we are, the more childishly and selfishly demanding we become. Even 'unselfish demanding' is selfish and can carry us away completely by its irresistible fascination. Repetitions of this process then become more frequent with the demands growing ever more unreasonable.

The tragedy is that we do not know what that cliff or the root is; so we do not know what to do and can only struggle back tooth and nail to the clifftop.

But what happens if the hand opens and lets go? Does that suggest suicide? It is unlikely that we physically will be in that situation. Now, I do not actually hang on such a cliff. Yet I may feel exactly as if I were when I desperately feel, 'I must have, or I'll die'. One wish only – that is the root. What happens if I relinquish that, let go of it? Try! A surprise awaits me: I cannot. It seems that root is me; everything else I'll give, let go, have given – this one I cannot be without! And without it I cannot be.

That is what needs to be broken, the attachment to 'I', identified as my wish/want. Life itself seems to have a vested interest in just that, so it hangs us onto the cliff. Religion and the principles of our cultural background suggest what is to be done, their teachings provide examples of it, and adherence to their precepts and principles develops the strength to actually bring it off, to open that clutching fist/heart and to plummet down.

The new life that is then found is a wider, fuller one – free of the anxiety of 'I must have or I'll die', free of 'I must get rid of or I can't live', free, in short, of all the 'I'-manifestations and 'I'-machinations that make life a long, suffering drudge. And then there is also much more time available to lend a helping hand or listening ear, to give a kind word or smile – not in some grand and abstract cause to come off sometime in the future, but here, now, with you, my neighbour and friend.

CHAPTER III
The One Way

24 *Step Carefully*

No portraits or sculptures existed of the Buddha. After he died, a great longing arose to know what he had looked like. Anybody who was ancient enough to have met him was sure of an attentive audience.

Just such a person was a nun, now over a hundred years old. To procure some solitude, she had moved out of the town into a little hermitage, but anyone wishing to enquire would soon come to hear of her. One day a sincere seeker, a highly attained elder monk, sent a message to her requesting a meeting. She agreed, but having her own ways of assessing her visitors, set up a large jar with water by the side of the rope curtain that functioned as the front door. The visitor arrived, pulled aside the curtain and, striding in, accidentally kicked over the jar. The nun scolded, 'There goes the greatly attained one, so exalted that he can't even keep from messing up this poor abode.' To the great credit of the Elder, who in rank certainly was well above the venerable nun, he apologized and entreated her to tell him about the Buddha.

The nun, well aware of this, now assured him, 'In spite of your carelessness, you deserve hearing the story and will profit by it. You see, my parents were devout followers of the Lord Buddha, and when he once again came to our neighbourhood to preach, they went there and took me with them. I was a flighty teenager not a bit interested in his teachings, but was content enough to come along all dressed up in my Sunday finery and pleased with my appearance.

A huge crowd had assembled and sat respectfully facing the Buddha. I hardly listened and soon got bored, but not daring to fidget, I began to play with my ornaments. Suddenly my hairpin, a family heirloom, worked loose and slithered down into the long grass out of sight. I was horror-struck; not daring to make a commotion, I surreptitiously searched as far as my hands could reach but, however I tried, the pin had vanished. I was in despair – what was I to do?

Suddenly I was aware of a radiance and looking up beheld the Buddha's eyes upon me. From between his eyes a ray shone directly in front of me and in its light I caught the sparkle of my pin in the long grass. With a sob I retrieved it and my heart turned. The World-Honoured One himself, preaching to such a large audience, had perceived the plight of an inattentive girl, fidgeting about, and yet had taken pity on her plight and compassionately helped her out of it. At that moment I knew that all I wanted was to devote myself to him and his teaching, and have done so ever since.'

The old nun smiled at the Elder and added, 'You see, if even the World-Honoured One was not above beholding a flighty girl's commotion about a lost hairpin and extended his kindness to help her, you might also exercise the same and not kick over my water jar again. So when you leave, step carefully, if you please.'

What a lesson! And what a story! We may take it personally: step carefully when you leave – carefully from now on. The Buddha's last words, 'Strive on heedfully', express the same message, the perennial teaching through the ages, the way to become truly human. Tread carefully! For this a change of heart is necessary, a change of attitude – to be careful of what is, no longer centred on 'I' and my concerns only. That is all – but what a long road it is towards just that, how different it is from what it first seemed and how manifold are its ramifications.

My gripes, resentments, fears, wants and hates fuel my own suffering as well as cause others to suffer. So we need to step carefully, to look out. This is not as simple as it seems hence the requirement of a true 'change of heart'. I cannot help being self-centred, just that is the nature of 'I'. And as long as I am self-centred, I cannot be truly careful – the bias is towards 'I', and this renders any attempt of 'I' to be selfless as absurd. Thus the dilemma that although I want to be selfless, to act carefully, I cannot do so; and the more I want and try to, the more I roll myself up into a tangle. The proverbial do-gooder and the compulsive busy-body are a warning to us all.

But then, how am I to step carefully? Do I need to be consciously aware of everything, watching myself all the time like a hawk? Well, however I try, I just cannot do it and only get ever more self-engrossed in the process.

We find the clue for how to step carefully in the Buddha's Teachings of selflessness (Anatta); so the understanding arises that, paradoxically, no 'I' can but No-I can! Our story highlights this aspect and describes the way towards it.

Essential for the start is a momentum, a change of heart, a being touched or moved deeply and thus a 'being turned around' as happened to the careless girl. From that change arises the wish or aspiration to strive towards that which moved, that quality or value which is felt to be more than I. This aspiration supplies the energy to undertake and maintain a practice directed towards that value. But the girl was fortunate; or it may be said that it was her good Karma that she met the Buddha, the All-Enlightened and All-Compassionate One, who from his own experience could spell out the Way.

In times like ours when most if not all true cultural and spiritual values have become obsolete, there is a dearth of 'those who know' and an abundance of those who loudly proclaim and try to sell their notion of salvation. Yet our hearts long for something and so we easily fall prone to any New Age cult or regress again into rigidifying selfishness. Charisma is a word frequently used today – yet perhaps the greatest sage of our century, Ramana Maharshi (not to be mistaken for the much later Maharishi) replied to the question of how to recognize a genuine teacher, that, 'in his presence you feel peace and calm.' How different from the usual incitement to do good or to instigate something for a communal cause or movement – vanity, all vanity! Such 'doing' inevitably leads to strife. Inner peace and calm is an attitude that arises in the cause of practice, and it spells true selflessness and thus goodwill in general. With that compassion develops, the care of heedfully walking through life, stepping out unhurriedly, carefully setting one foot at a time, hands gentle and eyes open, seeing and responding whole-heartedly from a heart that has itself become empty and at-one again. And now that it is made good, it is no longer under any compulsion to do good. Only such a heart is also truly creative. This is the message of the nun who knew the Buddha.

Just before dawn a Heavenly Being of wondrous radiance appeared to a monk and addressed him, 'Brother, this anthill smoulders by night and bursts into flame by day. Listen to this parable!

The Brahmin said, 'Dig, oh wise one, taking thy tool.' And the wise one took his tool and dug and came upon a crowbar, and said, 'Here is a crowbar.' Then said the Brahmin, 'Throw down the crowbar. Take thy tool, wise one, and dig.' And he did so and came upon a bladder, and said, 'Here is a bladder.' Then said the Brahmin, 'Throw down the bladder. Take thy tool and dig, wise one.' And he did so and came upon a two-pronged fork, and (in like manner) a casket, a tortoise, a knife blade, a lump of meat; in each case he was told by the Brahmin to throw it down and continue digging. Finally he came upon a snake. Then said the Brahmin, 'Let be the snake. Slay not the snake; do honour to the snake.'

'Now,' said the Heavenly Being, 'Ask the Exalted One, the Buddha, for an explanation of this parable for only he and those of his line can give one.' And having said so, he vanished.

When the night was gone, the monk approached the Exalted One, related what had happened and reverently asked, 'What, Lord, is the anthill? What is that which smoulders by night? What is that which bursts into flame by day? Who the Brahmin, who the wise one, what the tool, what the digging, what the crowbar, the bladder, the two-pronged fork, the casket, the tortoise, the knife blade, the lump of meat, and what the snake?'

'The anthill', said the Buddha, 'is this body – compounded of the four elements, begotten by parents, fed on rice and soup, impermanent, liable to destruction, of a nature to break up and to be scattered.

'And whatsoever, Brother, is thought over and pondered at night concerning one's daily needs, that is the smouldering by night. Whatsoever, Brother, after pondering and thinking it over by night, one puts into action by day in thought, word and deed, that is the bursting into flame by day.

'The Brahmin stands for the Tathagata, the Fully Awakened One. The wise one is a name for one who is yet a learner. The tool is a name for seeing.

'Digging means earnest application. The crowbar stands for delusion or ignorance. Throw away the crowbar purports the banishment of ignorance. "Dig, wise one", means, use your tool.

'The bladder is a name for anger and the state of being angry. Throw away the bladder means cast aside anger and the state of being angry; that is what, "Dig, wise one, taking your tool" indicates.

'The two-pronged fork, Brother, is the name for wavering. "Throw away the fork" means abandon wavering. The casket is the name for the Five Hindrances of sensual desire, ill will, sloth and torpor, worry and flurry, and doubting/hesitating. "Throw away the casket" means abandon the Five Hindrances. The tortoise stands for the Five Grasping Groups, of body, feeling, perception, intentional acts or impulses, and sense-consciousness. "Throw away the tortoise" means abandon the Five Grasping Groups. The knife blade is a name for the five strands of Sensual Delight, to wit:

of shapes perceived by the sense of sight, delightful pleasing, attractive, dear, pleasure-giving, and lustful. Likewise those perceived by the ear, the nose, the tongue, and those tangible by the body. "Throw away the knife blade" means abandon the five strands of Sensual Delight.

'The lump of meat stands for the Lust of Enjoyment. "Throw away the lump of meat" means abandon that.

'The snake, Brother, is a name for one who has destroyed the propensity of grasping (outflows). Let be the snake, slay not the snake, do honour to the snake – that is the meaning of it.'

This is the advice given to an aspirant of the religious life. But it is in the nature of universal truth that it is true at all levels, at all times, in all places, for everybody. In itself, truth is invisible, intangible – spirit, essence. Since the time of our beginning we human beings have dimly perceived it as an acting force, a 'something', and have ceaselessly occupied ourselves to render it perceptible, to somehow swaddle it up so as to give form to what in itself is nothing, to put a name to it so that it might be 'known.'

This truth also governs our ordinary life – its perennial laws apply and function whether we know it or not, and by what names we call it is irrelevant. The Parable of the Smouldering Anthill may also be looked at in terms of our ordinary, everyday life and help us to live it wholly as well as wisely.

What an apt analogy the anthill is for the body! Its overall structure, once it has grown up, holds for a span, yet is in continuous change internally as is the anthill. Moreover, this body, once it has come into existence is inevitably bound to cease to exist sooner or later. It is not morbid to reflect on this; rather, it gives some perspective and with that some purchase on the passions and obsessions that otherwise sway us completely. Not only the monk's cell and the philosopher's study but until not so long ago an educated man would have a skull in his room and underneath in beautiful lettering, usually in Latin, 'Remember death.'

Today we are frightened of death because we no longer reflect on our mortality, and the security of faith has also become obsolete. But there are signs of a return – the new hospice movement is but one of them. The media present the gory side of death – as far as looks go. But however sudden an accident, the old riding proverb reassures us, 'Between the saddle and the ground, mercy I sought and mercy found.' And as to the much more usual death 'from natural causes', as are illness and old age, preferably in familiar or friendly surroundings, the dignity and majesty of a dead face and its serenity, imprints itself and reassures rather than threatens. Life prepares us for death; but if we run away from life prompted by the fancies of our mind, death becomes a threat, and the faster we run, the more so. Then we lie awake at night, milling over how we can turn this to our advantage or avert that, planning this endlessly, and finally having to drug ourselves to sleep by means of a pill. Truly, the anthill smoulders by night – and bursts into flame by day when we hotly pursue our fantasies and chase gain and fame of one type or another. Our lives are becoming ever more hectic and noisy; who on coming home likes to sit down quietly in a comfortable chair, declutch from the demands of the job and the journey home, and just be there with and by themselves for a while? Who still feels this to be a necessity and is recharged by such a quiet spell? The benefit of this is known, but we no longer know how to do it. So some of us go to Yoga classes or learn to meditate or whatever, just to dampen the conflagration of that burning anthill.

The Brahmin in our parable stands for the Buddha. He, a man like us, by his own effort and aspiration, came to seeing things without the grasping outflows of personal attachment and aversion, thus saw things the way they really are – and may stand as the trusted guide to such seeing. Such perception takes out of life the hectic rush, the pressure and tension, and instead fills the human heart with understanding and warmth. These then flow out from it as friendliness and helpfulness, and are harmonious with what is. Moreover, as different from so many of our modern prophets, the Buddha never claimed that he had found anything new, only said he had 'rediscovered an ancient path that leads to an ancient city'. This ancient city is the human heart liberated from all excessive selfishness and with that also from isolation and fear. Perhaps this human heart is what we need to rediscover these days – the heart that is full of wisdom, with its clarity of seeing and for which intellectual cleverness and intentional ambition are no substitutes. Such a heart is compassionate rather than indulging in sloppy sentimentality or brutal aggression.

The Fully Awakened One is another appellation of the Buddha – the analogy being to someone who dreams of grievous suffering only to find himself on awakening comfortably in bed. The clever one will point out at once that it was only in a dream that he suffered. But to the dreamer himself, his suffering feels real. The Buddha is the guide out of this suffering

– but not the Buddha alone; so are all those, we are told, who have awakened to that same clear seeing, to the insight into the Way all things are, and thus also to the warmth of fellow-feeling and the strength and willingness to act out of that, to be of help and assistance to others.

The wise one in our parable is the aspirant, the one who has become aware of the burning and singeing qualities of the passions that drive, the ambitions that obsess, who feels that there is another life and more to life than 'just that'. This is the correct seeing which the guide tells him to put to work.

With that he can now set out to clear his vision and to develop a new and more harmonious attitude to and in his life. So starting on the road and commencing the digging, he comes first of all upon a crowbar, which, the parable tells us, stands for delusion or ignorance. In Buddhism this is a technical term, and is considered the basic obfuscation, the blinkers that obstruct us from seeing things as they are. Because self-centred, we are biased and so can see things only as they concern me, according to my opinions; these blinkered notions hold me in thrall. To clear one's vision is therefore of utmost importance not only for our own welfare but also for what we can contribute to that of others around us and thus to Life itself. References to 'another life', to being re-born or to awaken as from a dream, all refer to this change of heart, to the clear seeing which is also called 'seeing with the Single Eye'. Though such seeing is in itself entirely natural, we have become so deluded by our egoity and heedless notions that it takes time and dedicated endeavour to shed these habitual blinkers. The requirement for this to occur is nothing less than a transformation of the emotional energy itself because it is this energy which 'fires' our passionate wants, aversions and notions. The 'digging', however, is not a kind of self-analysis or continuous self-observation which would only strengthen egoity further; rather, it entails following a specific way or prescribed training in the process of which certain stages are passed through, certain discoveries are made and let go of – as metaphorically illustrated in our parable.

The next thing that emerges in this quest is a bladder, standing for anger and the state of being angry. Once the bladder's holding capacity has reached its limit, it bursts and splashes out. This is experienced as the compulsive urge to either procure and make 'my own' what is coveted, or annihilate what gives offence so as to make life endurable again! Hence these two 'drives' together with and consequential to the basic delusion (of an I as an independent, separate entity) are aptly called the 'Three Fires', their power expressed by the proverb that 'needs must when the devil drives'.

These Fires, the parable tells us, make our anthill flare by day; thus the aspirant is admonished to 'throw away anger and the state of being angry'. This, however, as we all know to our cost, is easier said than done. For example, a real burst of rage is not something I can lay down by an act of will – it has me rather than I it! Factually, I am carried away by it, have become it for the time being; it is now the anger that speaks and acts; even the voice changes and reason fails. The same applies, of course, also in the case of infatuation, the irresistible attraction of some object without which life is no longer worthwhile. Such obsession regresses to the prototype: facial and verbal expressions become stereotype, like lover's language or the accusations of anger and hate.

Once fully arisen, these Fires are of tremendous, even compelling force. As the passions that lead astray, desire, aggression and lust for power have always been known and feared yet were also felt to be the source of inspiration. Hence from of old their taming, gentling, their transformation has been striven for or at least their being kept in check. This is the purport behind tribal and other forms of law, of all reforms, customs, of all myths and religions, and is also behind the wearying labour of bringing up the young to become in their turn informed and responsible members of the community.

The need for the transformation of this inner force or psychic energy is so important and yet so little understood that an objective look at it seems indicated before going on with our parable which deals with just this transformation.

We all know the fierce flare of real rage or the power of an infatuation. We also know that we do not make them, they happen to us willy-nilly when we come in contact with an object that is seen as attractive or offensive; both have the power to hold us in thrall. We also know that thus 'fired' we are not capable of cool deliberation, reason has become inaccessible, idiomatically expressed as blinded by rage or lust.

Now, the energy in itself is neither good nor bad; it may be conceived of as life energy, in itself imperceptible, invisible, not a thing, yet animating all sentient beings, and is also the formative, ordering principle in inanimate matter; as that it 'in-forms' all forms.

Crystals, for example, 'grow' – that is, their structure arranges itself or 'forms' itself in concord with the properties of the constituents. These are specific to a given class of crystal, and so consequently is their interior structure, which fact has been employed in classifying them, by their 'habit' and the angles between developed 'faces'. But not only the 'faces', the atomic structure itself is orientated in specific ways, seemingly growing along axes of a seemingly three-dimensional framework. The angles these axes form with each other depend on this structure and for a given class are constant and accurate to the fraction of a degree – and yet, factually, such an axial system is purely assumed; in itself it 'is not', does not exist as such.

This 'ordering principle' functions as life energy in sentient beings, where it seems to make things grow, blossom, fruit all in their season – but again in itself 'is not'. 'The Dao that can be expressed is not the eternal Dao'.

The paradox is that what itself is no-thing should be a power of cosmic dimension, an elementary force, bipolar in its action – expressed in Buddhism neutrally as 'coming to be and ceasing to be', but seen in Western conception as the struggle between creation and destruction, between light and dark, good and evil. Buddhists see this as the Law of Change, ensuring that nothing can be permanent or remain the same for ever. It heaps up mountains, dries up oceans; it makes the snowdrops grow and open in their season, whatever the weather; it makes birds hatch out their eggs and feed their young; pairs male and female to bring forth the next generation – and the next. To behold it all in awe and wonder, to contribute one's mite, yes – but without clinging to such shifting sands.

As with the axial system of the crystal, it is we who postulate such a thing as a structuring principle, and then picture it as 'some-thing' (God, gods, divine will, intelligent universe, life force, etc.). We then conceive it as a 'doer', when in fact there is no such thing. And the wonder, the miracle is that although 'no-thing' in itself, yet according to this airy 'no-thing' all things manifest qualities which, being inherent, also account for their different forms, i.e. their appearance according to their specific composition or structure. Hit hard enough, stone will shatter; but wood will splinter.

We may thus come to realize what in Buddhism is considered the 'basic delusion': first to assume a something when there is nothing; and then to ascribe 'intentional', self-directed, willful action to this hypothetical something! Does an echo perhaps reverberate here about the embargo against the making of graven images?

But how can such an arch-delusion have come about? It is peculiar to us human beings with our reflective consciousness. Who ever owned, or perhaps better was owned by, a cat, will know that a cat, with unerring certainty and determination, will find and occupy the warmest spot when cold, the coolest spot in hot weather, and invariably also the best chair, cushion, etc. But the cat does not do this by intellect or conscious purpose, nor does it have to search for 'the' spot; it just responds to the situation according to its inherent nature which informs it, as it does all forms – all being part of and making up 'what is'. An ant will always, under all circumstances, act as an ant, neither like a cat nor like a grasshopper.

What then has gone wrong with us that we have lost touch with this inherent awareness? Back to the cat; should it find that the best chair, warmest spot, etc., is occupied by me, or someone else, it will either jump on my lap or find the next best place; should the 'somebody else' be discovered to be of lower rank, the cat will attempt to dislodge him and occupy the desirable place or come to share it. What it will not do is to plan and campaign for it – to keep at it with ever-increasing annoyance and frustration, keep on manipulating how to nevertheless occupy that spot. It merely single-mindedly keeps its attention on it and waits its chance!

What is it that makes us human beings different? What produces tension and pressure? In this we can see the activities of all the Three Fires: the insistence on getting that desired spot for myself, the purposeful campaign to get rid of the offending occupier that prevents 'my' possession of the desired spot, the intentional, determined pursuit of this 'my' chosen aim, and 'my' frustration and resentment if thwarted.

Now, as to 'my chosen aim', careful investigation reveals some surprising insights. Like the cat, like all forms, we naturally accord with what is, are in harmony with the inherent principle, conform to it. This conformity itself, as with the cat, assures for the individual the best position within the given circumstance. Hence we are again reminded that this basic principle has structuring properties which govern both the individual within a species such as pecking and grazing orders, ranking, etc., as well as the behaviour patterns of a species on contact with others. Some of these patterns are innate in the species – as when a tiny duckling hatched out by a hen serenely sails out on a sheet of water while mother hen screeches in despair! Other patterns are imprinted on first sight, as the newly-hatched duckling or gosling attaches itself to whatever it sees first. Still other such patterns have to be taught to become imprinted, as a cat teaches her kittens to chase, catch, and play with what moves, which in the wild cat is the hunting skill.

Preferences for food, position, etc., are the norm. With us, however, this pattern has become distorted and biased as the focus shifted from the dictates of the situation: such as lean and abundant seasons, migrational wanderings after food supplies, juggling for place within the community. With these diminishing, they were replaced by manipulating in a purely self-interested way. Such a relentlessly self-interested behaviour pattern has, to begin with, great advantages for the individual and profits the species; we are all aware of it and foster it. Unfortunately, however, and we are only becoming aware of this now, and this trend seems to be taking on logarithmic proportions in its insatiable demands for 'more, more – better, better – faster, faster.'

How can we best picture the beginnings of such an ego-centric new trend that irrevocably changes the world we live in, and threatens to destroy it? Reflecting consciousness differs from sense-consciousness such as seeing, hearing, etc., not only by perceiving and ordering sense perceptions but also of thoughts including thoughts of itself, i.e. it can reflect on itself. Now, once reflecting consciousness begins to develop, with its conscious perception of the natural preferences of a given body, a whole new mode of perception comes into being. Constant picking and choosing is the natural order of life and governs adapting to circumstances. But now it is deflected from the situation and takes on a new focus and centre, as an active and choosing doer. Because of the constant activity of choosing, this doer seems to be constant.

Thus the misconception (delusion) of an intentional actor who controls individual response. With this is born the delusion of an independent 'I' who, now prompted by 'my' preferences, is consciously choosing and going after this my choice. This occasions the shift away from the one-ness with the situation (paradise), leaving a separate, struggling, scheming 'I' (labouring in the sweat of my brow), an 'I' that holds what is not 'I' cheap or fears it. Moreover, the delusion of being separated out of the living context makes for loneliness. Consequently nowadays we are concerned with lack of communication, fear and insecurity, the unpleasant perceptions of which I attempt to drown in a cacophony of sense-stimulants, noise, and ever-increasing rush. Thus driven, I am willy-nilly the shuttlecock of the great forces of life which, because unlived, turn destructive. 'Inherent information', our inheritance and birthright, seems inaccessible; yet, somehow, stubbornly, the heart intuits that there must be something – else or more – and hankers after it.

It follows that for a conscious re-linking (re-ligio) of the part (I) with the whole (Life), a full turnaround or change of heart is required. The basic energy, life-power, whatever called, has been allowed to regress almost to its primeval state. With law and order no longer esteemed, with most if not all cultural values obsolete and religious values lost, an ever-increasing barbarism seeks to despoil all that was held dear or respected in the human realm.

In itself, the elementary state of the bipolar sway of energy is neither good nor bad, but in its primary manifestation makes short shrift of human endeavour. A mountain range erupting in volcanic activity and splitting half a continent, sea flooding in and covering what was land – these are usual occurrences on our restless planet. But as we know, in our human world and surroundings, such elementary eruptions work grievous harm on all planes.

How can we then effect the necessary change from our present state towards a true transformation of these forces that have turned negative for us, have become destructive because of our relentless and heedless pursuit of I, me, mine gain, profit, fame, notions, theories, opinions, convictions?

In our parable, this is the bladder and the injunction, 'throw away the bladder'. As interpreted to the dreamer by the Buddha, this stands for 'cast away anger and the state of being angry'. We get angry when our will is crossed; much devoted effort is necessary for this casting away as is explicitly detailed in the further instructions; hence the 'dig further, wise one, use your tool.'

The wise aspirant of this great endeavour obeys and continues digging. He next comes upon a two-pronged fork. The Buddha, as the aspirant's inherent information or wisdom, explains that it stands for hesitating, wavering, the familiar horns of the dilemma of 'should I or should I not?' In a way I want to continue, in a way I don't. Is it worth it – is it all a hoax? How often are we in such a dilemma, counting pros and cons, and cannot make up our mind or rush and regret it. Or the conflict is between a raging passion and at least the vestiges of conscience or reason. To endure such conflicts until 'ripened' and not be carried away entails real suffering, a patient endurance without budging, and yet all the while carrying out the usual daily chores and occupation. Just this is the transforming agent which bit by bit gentles the elementary power of the passions, humanizes them as it were.

An analogy for that, a favourite one in Zen Buddhism, is to liken the elementary energy to a totally wild but magnificent bull, dangerous in his power and quite unpredictable, governed only by his lusts and stubborn self-will. The task to be undertaken is to gentle this bull, not just to tame him and make him obedient – and bulls do not lend themselves to even that – but to actually gentle his nature. Working with the bull, with the passions themselves and their overwhelming power entails enduring them rather than being carried away by them. Enduring means 'living them' without giving in to them. Any active struggling or opposing them head-on only lends them further power. Pursued with diligence, this will effect a genuine gentling. The two-pronged fork, with the transformation being in progress and there being no more wavering, now has fulfilled its purpose. Hence the advice is, 'Take up your tool, wise one, and dig.' And the wise one obeys.

Next he comes upon a casket which the Buddha likens to the Five Hindrances still lurking under what seemed almost accomplished. There are frequent warnings against being deceived or deceiving oneself into believing one is 'beyond' the sway of the emotions, while merely having trained oneself to keep 'cool'. But underneath such artificial blandness there is a veritable snake's nest of notions, opinions, views, convictions – unconscious yet in constant need of being aired and affirmed or else it harbours bitter resentment and strikes with deadly venom. In that form it is subtler and more deadly than the red-hot passions of the flesh. Hence the necessity of a detailed examination of what still lurks in the hidden depths, only too ready to flare up with undiminished strength. Such probing demands painstaking and humble application, going over the same ground again and again. Hence the diligent digging further until the casket may be truly abandoned.

This is not yet the end, for, 'Throw away the casket, take up your tool, wise one, and dig', we are admonished. Unless truly cast away, the contents of the casket are hindrances for any further digging – the tangled skein of greed/want, ill will, sloth and torpor or as we now call it, diminishing attention span due to the atrophying power of application. Worry and flurry keep me busy with myself and with inessentials but make me run ever faster avoiding an encounter with myself – the radio in the car, heavy metal music and raves being recent favourites. And the nagging doubt, part envy part demand – I want to believe but cannot, and even my own convictions are not always convincing. Accordingly, although that casket seems already abandoned, further digging reveals remnants to be eradicated by means of transformation.

What then next appears is a tortoise which stands for the Five Grasping Groups, of form/body, feeling/sensation, conception/discerning, volitional impulses, and sense-consciousness – each with their specific graspings, and attachments. In Buddhism these are known as the Five Aggregates which make up the human individual with no 'I' to be found or indeed necessary for their functioning. As that, they are in harmony, that is in accord with the nature of all that is, being of the same nature. Should, however, the delusion of a self-centred 'I' arise, with its egocentric preferences and aversions, the volitional impulses will wrench the whole bundle out of its natural accord and so put it under considerable stress. Moreover, all such ego-centric, 'I'-biased striving for ever more, better, faster, is eventually unattainable, and only causes disappointments and frustration, in short suffering. Each of the strands of the bundle themselves have attachments and aversions – the body with its senses, the feelings of what is pleasant and desirable and what is not, notions and opinions indulged in and firmly held or contested. Fired by this fictitious 'I' they give rise to impulsive, hasty, unskillful actions which are productive of further Karma. This then adds to the endless thought-streams, planning courses of action, resurrecting past resentments and producing all kinds of internal picture-shows. Somebody jogging with the Walkman clamped over the ears, or driving the car with the radio blaring, is incapable of being in and with what is, or of enjoying their own company for a bare ten minutes. Truly, we are restlessly driven by the Fires reflected in these Five Grasping Groups. The message comes across, does it not, 'Throw away the tortoise, take your tool, wise one, and dig!'

The tortoise is an apt symbol. A reptile, much older in the evolutionary chain than we with our warm mammalian blood that easily boils or throbs with carnal lusts and obsessions about powers and dominions. All this is alien to the reptile, the snake – itself cold-blooded and needing to be warmed by outside conditions. Dangerous, and striking like lightning, it was once considered immortal because it sloughs off its skin; unless you kill it, you rarely find a dead snake. Added to all this there is then the wisdom of the serpent, that other power older than and alien to our cerebral consciousness, inaccessible to it yet life-enhancing in its power. Achievement, civilization, culture, potential for the future, are all nourished from this tremendous power-house. And so encapsulated in this serpent, encoded in its genes as we now tend to call it, is also all the wisdom of life itself. Our developing cerebral, reflective consciousness has lost contact with the 'old' brain, can no longer decipher and does not encompass it. This is what the wisdom of the serpent stands for. Much further training is needed to realize this wisdom in the human context.

The Indian concept of the coiled Kundalini serpent, aroused and made to ascend along specific stages/centres, is another symbolic representation of the transformation of this elemental, a-human power into full humanity. In some Yoga systems this is beautifully portrayed by the loop, that is at the highest point of spiritual transfiguration: at the top of the head it is seen to turn over and flow down to the level of the (human) heart with its inherent warmth and understanding, which is now liberated and can act freely out of its own nature.

From now on there is no more backsliding; the pull is irreversibly forward and cannot again regress to the merely biological. But the tortoise has to be left behind and the digging has to continue because just at this point, with the heart touched, it needs to be made absolutely sure that no trace of egoity remains. With so much power now having become free, if misdirected, the process can go drastically wrong. In the language of the Bull-herding Pictures, the bull needs to be genuinely gentled, the elemental energy itself has to become human. If the digging, the gentling work, was not thorough enough, was too hurried or too coveted, then the outcome is a catastrophe, 'Man Vanished, Bull

Remains'. We all have met minor types of such bull-men or bull-women; history, both worldly and religious, documents their perennial arising and perdition. What they all have in common is that even with best intentions, they carry a train of destruction in their wake – and are themselves deeply unhappy. In European knightly epics the 'black knight' is invincible because he has forsworn true love, the humanizing quality. Alberich and Hagen in Wagner's 'Ring Cycle' are good examples of this type and how they work their own destruction.

'Throw away the tortoise', that is, abdicate from power, wise one, and go on digging! And look at what is found next – a knife blade! Which, as the Buddha explains, is a name for the five strands of Sensual Delight, dear and attractive forms (eyes), sounds (ears), smells (nose), taste (tongue) and touch (body); and because dear and pleasant, attachment and craving for repetition arises and, if gratified, the itch for further and ever further titillations. But should the dear and pleasant fail to continue like unrequited love, it is like a knife turning in the heart, is it not? Moreover, dear and pleasant and even if painful still dear, is life to me, and death is feared like the naked blade that cuts it off. Just that binds the delusion, 'me', into continuation; so in spite of all the work done there is still an underlying stratum that even the 'old serpent' cannot reach. To sever that, the blade is needed.

Four characteristics have to be outworn and have to fall off for truly completing the transformation, so that the notion of an 'I' may be utterly outgrown; only then can the 'other life' commence. Does the butterfly remember his being a caterpillar? Nor can the caterpillar envisage the state and life of the butterfly he is 'destined', 'programmed', bound to become, to develop into by the force of the law inherent in him as well as in the universe.

We have wilfully ('my way') sprung ourselves out of this given context of evolution and so need to find or re-discover our way, not back into but forward towards it, which demands dedicated effort. Again, the knife blade that cuts through the knots of ignorance, through all fond delusions and arrogant notions, in short through three of the four characteristics that make up me: I, a person (human), a sentient being (somebody). But there it usually sticks; the fourth (a life) is not yet quite transformed.

Hence, digging on, wisely, a lump of flesh is come upon as the last vestige of clinging to what is deludedly conceived of as I, me, mine, as what 'I must have to live!' Let go of that, too, and dig on, wise one! Let go of this final clinging to a 'mine', 'my' life, without which I am no-thing. And dig on.

And now, with this basic delusion gone for good, what Master Hakuin calls 'The Great Death' has died and another life opens.

But, although opened, it has not yet been entered into and cannot be engaged in because still more work is needed for the transformation to be complete and the completion itself to become conscious awareness. So, take up your tool, wise one, and dig.

What is now encountered, lo and behold, is the serpent again, but no longer the 'old' snake as symbolized by the tortoise, but the winged serpent, the Naga, which in Far Eastern representation is the dragon who holds the pearl of wisdom in his claw representing totality. And this is now accessible and amenable to the dedicated seeker who in his great endeavour has rediscovered that pearl – and himself – in his own heart.

The Western hero sees the dragon as a dreaded enemy and on encounter is quick to slay him – only to come to a sticky end himself not long after! Why? The dragon-power dangerously inflates his 'I' and so his own hubris works his undoing. Whereas in the symbolism and insight of the East, the sage, usually old and mellow after long endeavour, has shed 'I' and self-centredness and hence is without fear. Now he can associate with the dragon and so shares in the dragon-power and wisdom. Therefore the ascending affirmation may be read as, 'Let be the snake. Slay not this serpent. Do honour to the dragon.' With that, the old enmity has come to an end. The serpent, redeemed and yielding its wisdom, ensures that what has been attained remains here where our feet stand and its compassionate understanding is made available for the benefit of all who come into its ambience.

May all beings be happy, may all attain Buddhahood!